STORIES OF WOMEN
WRECKED BY LOVE

LIFEWISE BOOKS

JESUS GIRL
STORIES OF WOMEN WRECKED BY LOVE

Scriptures marked CEV are taken from the CONTEMPORARY ENGLISH VERSION (CEV): Scripture taken from the CONTEMPORARY ENGLISH VERSION copyright© 1995 by the American Bible Society. Used by permission.

Scriptures marked KJV are taken from the KING JAMES VERSION (KJV): KING JAMES VERSION, public domain.

Scriptures marked NIV are taken from the NEW INTERNATIONAL VERSION (NIV): Scripture taken from THE HOLY BIBLE, NEW INTERNATIONAL VERSION®. Copyright© 1973, 1978, 1984, 2011 by Biblica, Inc.™. Used by permission of Zondervan

Scriptures marked NKJV are taken from the NEW KING JAMES VERSION (NKJV): Scripture taken from the NEW KING JAMES VERSION®. Copyright© 1982 by Thomas Nelson, Inc. Used by permission. All rights reserved.

Scriptures marked ESV are taken from the THE HOLY BIBLE, ENGLISH STANDARD VERSION (ESV): Scriptures taken from THE HOLY BIBLE, ENGLISH STANDARD VERSION® Copyright© 2001 by Crossway, a publishing ministry of Good News Publishers. Used by permission.

Scriptures marked NLT are taken from the HOLY BIBLE, NEW LIVING TRANSLATION (NLT): Scriptures taken from the HOLY BIBLE, NEW LIVING TRANSLATION, Copyright© 1996, 2004, 2007 by Tyndale House Foundation. Used by permission of Tyndale House Publishers, Inc., Carol Stream, Illinois 60188. All rights reserved. Used by permission.

Scripture quotations marked TPT are from The Passion Translation®. Copyright© 2017, 2018 by Passion & Fire Ministries, Inc. Used by permission. All rights reserved. ThePassionTranslation.com.

Published by:

 LIFEWISE BOOKS

PO BOX 1072
Pinehurst, TX 77362
LifeWiseBooks.com

To contact JESUS Girl, email: Jesusgirl.us@gmail.com

ISBN (Print): 978-1-952247-15-6
ISBN (Ebook): 978-1-952247-16-3

DEDICATION

From Nia:

As I was writing, the Lord said to me, "Dedicate this book to your granny. She was an original Jesus Girl". He also showed me a picture of her. In that moment, I understood exactly what God meant. As a child, I was raised by my mother, father and my granny, living between the three of them.

On the weekends at my granny's house, we got up early before the sun came up and went to her garden where she grew a little of everything like corn, peas, tomatoes, potatoes, squash and greens. We went with our garden tools to collect the ripe produce to bring back home to shuck, pick, separate, and clean. We would then jump in the car to share the produce with many other families. I now understand my granny was teaching reaping and sowing. She put seed in the ground and received a harvest to nourish her family as well as others. She worked her gardens for as long as I can remember.

She was also big on giving her tithe to the Lord. I knew, even as little child, that a dime out of every dollar belonged to God before I spent anything. She also taught me that the tithe is holy, so set it aside and don't touch it!

The most important thing my granny did for me was to introduce me to Jesus Christ. Yes, of course, we went to church literally every day. She was the epitome of servanthood. She served her friends, strangers, her church, her pastor, and first lady. She was willing and available to be used by God. She even cut the grass at the church on occasion.

As a result of her giving and servanthood, I watched God provide for her time and time again. She didn't have to buy a house or a car because God always gave them to her, fully paid for. The most valuable lessons I've learned were from her, so I dedicate this book to my granny, Tommie D. Williams, an original Jesus Girl.

October 25, 1927 - October 21, 2014

CONTENTS

CONTACT US:

Jesus Girl LLC
P.O. Box 454
O'Fallon, IL 62269
844-469-2326
Jesusgirl.us@gmail.com
Jesusgirlus.com

INTRODUCTION

Where did the idea of Jesus Girls come from? The authors of this book are Jesus Girls, a group of prophetic business women each with their own unique story of what God has done for them. They know that what has been placed inside them is there to encourage other women to step up and follow Jesus with their whole heart and life. These Jesus Girls operate in supernatural healing and travel the world expanding God's kingdom with a message of deliverance, miracles, signs and wonders from their neighborhoods to the nations.

You may wonder, "Why would they call themselves Jesus Girls when they are women?"

Here's how Nia Owens answers that question:

> One day I had a dream where I saw specific ladies standing in a room with small black Bibles held to their chest, pressed against their hearts. The Lord said that each of these women would select a woman from the Bible and minister to the people about that woman's life.
>
> God showed me the faces of each woman that was to speak, and I knew I was to host a conference. I asked each of the ladies if they agreed to be in the conference and with no hesitation, everyone agreed. At that time, I didn't know what

to call the conference, so I asked the Lord, and within a week He answered. He said, "Jesus Girl". I knew He was answering my question about the conference, so I asked to clarify, "Jesus' girl?" And he said "No, Jesus Girl."

Since then God has taken what began as a vision and a stand-alone conference, to a book and now a movement. We continue to hold Jesus Girl conferences wherever God calls us, and this book is an act of obedience to the Lord to help bring the heart of Jesus Girl to the world.

But what makes a Jesus Girl different from someone who is simply saved by grace through Jesus Christ? A Jesus Girl is surrendered and committed to the call of God. She has made Jesus not only Savior but has also made Him Lord. When Jesus is your Lord, you're not just a hearer of the Word, but a doer. You live a life of obedience to God and are willing to lay down your life for Him, daily.

She has been brought out of the darkness and into the marvelous light. A Jesus Girl allows God to change her, wash, mold, and shape her into the image of Christ. She is not just talking the talk but walking the walk of God. She is not content settling for a normal life but wants the supernatural life God intended her to have. She is willing to go all the way with Jesus, including dying to her flesh so that Christ can live in and through her.

A Jesus Girl is committed to edify, heal, deliver, and set the captives free. She lifts her sister up and doesn't tear her down. She is a builder, encourager, and giver. She can say, "I'm not there yet but I'm striving to be". A Jesus Girl may get knocked down but won't stay down. She will get up and fight again. She is someone who makes mistakes but is willing to repent and turn around. She doesn't live in shame. She quickly forgives others and herself from sin and regret.

Now ask yourself, "Am I a Jesus Girl?"

In this book, you will be taken on a journey through the lives of eight women from the Bible who God gives us as powerful examples of Jesus Girls.

CHAPTER 1

Leah

CONFESSIONS OF
THE UNLOVED

HAVE IT ALL

Have you ever been around someone who seems to have it all? They are attractive, physically fit, managing a career and children all while being the perfect spouse. I know a few of those people. Whenever I'm around them, they talk about their perfect kids, their amazing spouse, how they made a costume for the school play, baked brownies for their child's class and still found time to get a promotion on their job and plan a romantic trip with their spouse.

I cringe when I am around these types because they appear to "have it all". I am the total opposite which made me question what "having it all" really means. My kids aren't perfect. I have to work hard at keeping my weight down. On my best day, my hair is in a messy bun and after merely giving my husband a peck on the cheek, I manage to barely make it out of the house to dash off to my small cubicle where no big deals or promotions are anywhere in sight. This is the reality of my life and the life of many women who want to "have it all".

What does "having it all" look like to you?

This reminds me of a great story of desire, disappointment, and redemption found in the Bible. It's the story of Leah in Genesis 29:16.

TRICKERY & THEFT

Our story starts with Jacob who was Abraham's grandson. One day after Jacob and his twin brother, Esau, had a fight, Jacob stole his brother's birth right by fooling his father into thinking he was Esau. Jacob's mother encouraged him to flee the land before Esau could kill him for his treachery. Jacob headed out to find a wife from a neighboring city where he knew family was located. (Gen. 28:6-9) When Jacob arrived in Haran, he came to a well where some of the townspeople were waiting to water their sheep and goats. Jacob talked with some of the folks there and asked if they knew a man named Laban (his uncle) and they said, "Yes." At that moment, Laban's daughter, Rachel, came to the well to water her father's flock. She was a shepherd.

When Jacob saw Rachel who was very beautiful, he went over to the well and single handedly moved the large stone so the flock could drink. Jacob went to Rachel, kissed her and wept aloud, telling her that he was her cousin, the son of her aunt Rebekah. Rachel ran to tell her dad who came quickly to meet Jacob. After Jacob stayed with Laban for a month, "Laban said to him, 'You shouldn't work for me without pay just because we are relatives. Tell me how much your wages should be.'"[1]

Jacob didn't ask Laban for a specific wage. Instead, Jacob volunteered to work for seven years in exchange for Rachel's hand in marriage.

"Now Laban had two daughters. The older daughter was named Leah, and the younger one was Rachel."[2] The Bible says that Leah had weak eyes. Some versions of the Bible say there was no sparkle in her eyes, some describe her as dull, tangled-eyed (cross-eyed), but nevertheless, it's clear she was nothing special to look at.

When it came to Rachel, the Bible is clear about her looks, saying she "...had a beautiful figure and a lovely face."[3] Rachel seemed to have it all. It was love at first sight for Jacob and "...he told her father, 'I'll work for you for seven years if you'll give me Rachel, your younger daughter, as my wife.'" "'Agreed!' Laban replied. 'I'd rather give her to you than to anyone else...'"[4] Jacob worked for seven years just to pay for Rachel. "But his love for her was so strong that it seemed to him but a few days."[5]

Finally, the time came for the wedding. "'I have fulfilled my agreement,' Jacob said to Laban. 'Now give me my wife so I can sleep with her.' So, Laban invited everyone in the neighborhood and prepared a wedding feast."[6] But that night, after a day of eating and drinking, when it was dark, Laban swapped daughters and sent in a veiled Leah to spend the wedding night with Jacob. When Jacob woke up in the morning to discover it was Leah, he was furious and yelled at Laban, "I worked seven years for Rachel! Why have you tricked me?"[7] Jacob, who had earlier tricked his own brother out of his birthright, had been tricked by his uncle. Laban said, "It's not our custom here to marry off a younger daughter ahead of the firstborn." "'But wait until the bridal week is over; then we'll give you Rachel, too—provided you promise to work another seven years for me.' So, Jacob agreed to work seven more years."[8] A week after he was married to Leah, he was given Rachel too. And the Bible says that Jacob loved Rachel and not Leah. (Gen. 29:30)

COMPARISON BREEDS LOW SELF-ESTEEM

Leah looked at Rachel as the one who had it all. Rachel was the chosen one. Rachel had the respect and the beauty. Leah was used by her father, disrespected by Jacob and taken for granted by Rachel. Leah's ultimate desire was to be loved yet she was not.

Can you imagine how Leah felt to give her virginity to a man and his response was basically, "What are you doing here?" He went to her father and said, "I don't want her! I want Rachel."

That had to be a devastating blow to her self-esteem. Where could she turn to be consoled? Certainly not her father who tricked someone into marrying her because he didn't think she could get a man on her own. Surely, she wouldn't receive consolation from her sister who was now in competition with her for the same man's attention. And to make matters worse, she bore Jacob's children with hope to gain his love and respect. Her efforts were not successful. She was a wife without her husband's love. Her disappointment must have been overwhelming

When all of your efforts and sacrifices aren't returned or appreciated, it is so hurtful. I think we can all agree that unreciprocated love is one of the worst feelings imaginable. The pain of becoming attached to someone in a way that isn't mutual can be traumatizing. False hope only leads to pain and continuous disappointment. Not only is putting time and effort into a person who doesn't love you unfair, it can also be the major obstacle standing in the way of finding true love with someone who is capable of loving you.

Leah gave Jacob several children. After the birth of each child, she hoped that he would love her, but that never happened. The Bible never says that Leah was envious of Rachel, but I am sure she felt some resentment. No matter how many children she had for Jacob, he loved and honored Rachel. The plot thickens because Rachel was barren and could not produce a child for Jacob. The unattractive one is fertile and the beautiful one is barren. Look at how this plays out. Can you relate to Leah's frustration of desire and desperation for love, acceptance, and respect from her family?

UNLOVED & UNDERVALUED

At some point in our lives, we have all been a version of Leah. Leah's insecurities make her relatable because we all desire to be loved. To many of us "having it all" looks like the perfect spouse, the perfect children, house, job, car and, of course, to be loved. We associate success with all those things mentioned but very few times have I ever heard people mention or equate their relationship with God as a part of their successful accomplishments.

The Bible clearly describes Leah's physical features and her slim chance to find love. The Bible is also clear that no one thought much of her. We've all felt unappreciated and undervalued sometime in our lives. Many women and men are in Jacob and Leah's position today. They are not together because of love. Some are together for financial reasons, stability, children or other motives. But nothing to do with love. Leah couldn't change her past, she couldn't change her husband, however she could change herself.

What are you doing about life challenges?

Are you bitter and desperate or are you willing and ready to give your burdens to God?

LEAH'S PROCESS

Let's step back and take a look at Leah's childbearing period when God began to do a work in her. "And when the Lord saw that Leah was hated, he opened her womb: but Rachel was barren."[9]

God opened Leah's womb and allowed her to become a mother before Rachel. This gave Leah the greatest status a woman in that society could have. Nevertheless, her longing for her husband to love her remained the primary goal in her mind. Her first three sons, Reuben, Simeon, and Levi were all named in hopes that her affection would not remain ignored. During those times, it was customary to name the children based on your state of mind or current situation.

Leah used Hebrew words that expressed her longing for Jacob. Leah gave birth to her first child, a boy, who she named Reuben. Reuben means, "To see" and she thought, "Now maybe my husband will see me; maybe I won't be invisible anymore." She had a second son and named him Simeon, which has to do with hearing: "Now maybe my husband will finally listen to me." But he didn't. She had a third son and named him Levi, which means "to be attached," and she said, "Maybe finally my husband's heart will be attached to me."

FINDING TRUE LOVE

Every time she had a child, Leah put all of her hopes in the possibility her husband would love her. She made an idol out of her husband and the thought of his love, but she still called on God. In verse 32, it says, "And Leah conceived and bore a son, and she called his name Reuben, for she said, 'Because the LORD has looked upon my affliction....'"[10] In the midst of her idolatry of love, she somehow managed to reach out to God. She finally started to get it. She said, "God can help me save myself through childbearing. God can help me save myself by getting my husband's love. So, she is using God, yet also acknowledging God. She is beginning to get it, and what is interesting is that, at the very end, something happens.

The first time she gives birth she says, "Now maybe my husband will see me. Now maybe my husband will love me." And when she gives birth to her third son, she says, "Now this time my husband will become attached to me..."[11] She conceived for the fourth time, and when she gave birth to Judah, she said, "This time!" Her response is totally different, no mention of husband, no mention of child. She says, "*This time* I will praise the Lord."[12]

At this point, she finally took her heart's deepest hopes off of her husband and her children and she put them in the Lord. Something happened to Leah; God did something in her. There was a breakthrough. She began to understand what you are supposed to do with your desire for one true love. She turned her heart toward the only true thing, the only real lover who can satisfy those needs. She finally turns to God.

Leah thought because Rachel was beautiful that she had it all but truthfully God blessed Leah beyond her comprehension. The unfortunate things that happened to Leah were not meant to destroy her but to make her draw nearer to God. Just like Leah, when challenges come, we try to fix the problem or change the situation ourselves, but God is waiting for us to cast our cares on Him.

THE LESSON OF LEAH

What we can learn from Leah is how to keep pushing through even when we are disappointed. This is hard because when we are disappointed repeatedly, we want to give up. We want to give up after the first disappointment. Most couldn't endure what Leah went through. The best decision Leah made was to give God praise. I'm not sure about you but when I place my thoughts on God, there is a sense of joy and peace that comes over me. The thought of God always makes me render a grateful "Hallelujah!"

God is worthy to be praised even through our disappointments. God often chooses to uplift the underdog, the rejected, or the unloved. We see that example in the life of Leah. God chose Leah to birth six of the twelve tribes of Israel. Leah gave God praise after the birth of Judah. Just look at how God turned things around for Leah. If you are ever in a place of feeling unloved and unwanted, know that God loves you and will raise you up in His time.

LEAH'S LINEAGE

What is interesting is that Jesus came from Leah's lineage through Judah, and Jesus also went through feeling unwanted and ultimately rejected. He was born in a manger and had no beauty that we would desire him. He came to his own people and they didn't receive him. At the end, nobody wanted Him. Everyone abandoned Him but God. Why did God allow this? He allowed it for you and for me. God sacrificed His Son so that we could have eternal life.

We don't always understand what God is doing but it's not for us to understand. We just have to have faith and give God what's due Him, our praise. You don't become closer to God through perfection. You become closer to God through weakness, through vulnerability, through trials and tests. God is showing us that He's always there through everything as we build our faith and trust Him. Leah taught me that having it all looks exactly like loving God!

My name is Andrea Hunt,
and I am a JESUS Girl.

Andrea Hunt is a minister at Christ for All Nations Church, Belleville Illinois. She's a wife, mother, business owner and corporate executive. Andrea has many degrees, certifications and awards, however her proudest accomplishment by far is becoming a minister of the gospel and sharing about God's unfailing love. She is passionate about the needs of the homeless and can often be found downtown handing out blankets and praying with the homeless. Andrea is proudly married to Terry Hunt, together they have five sons. She is the bragging and picture-sharing "Gigi" of six grandchildren.

CHAPTER 2
Hannah
TRUST & BELIEVE

WHY DO WE WANT WHAT WE WANT?

Have you ever desired something for a long time? Perhaps, it was a desire for a certain position or job, to live in a certain neighborhood, to drive a certain type of automobile, to attend a certain school, to get married or to have children. As long as there is human life, there will always be desires. The question is why do we want what we want?

There is a story in the Bible about a woman named Hannah. Her story is one that many women can relate to today. Hannah's name means grace and favor; however, her path in life seemed more like being overlooked or forgotten. She wanted to be a good wife and mother; however, she was barren.

WHY DID HANNAH WANT A CHILD?

In Hannah's day, it was humiliating and even considered a disgrace for a married woman to not bear children, specifically a son or sons. During that time, women were often shunned by other women, ostracized by their husbands and maybe even returned to their father's house because of their inability to conceive a child. Some women may even have been accused of having committed some "unforgivable sin" that angered God thus causing Him to punish them or curse them with infertility.

Today, many women have stories very similar to Hannah's. There are countless women that have agonized within themselves and or prayed for years about a certain desire they have, yet it is as if heaven hasn't heard their cries and petitions.

What happens when you have prayed persistently yet haven't received while others are progressing and moving forward? Women often celebrate the accomplishments of their sisters and sister friends. Birthdays, graduations, jobs, getting married, buying their first home, having children and even overcoming a terminal illness are all great reasons to get excited.

But what happens when those same women turn around and judge a member of their group because she has not received her heart's desire? Hannah likely heard things like, "God is angry with you because you have not been obedient", or "You must have sinned", or "You just don't have the faith needed to get what you want."

WHAT DID HANNAH DO WHEN HER ADVERSARY CAME AGAINST HER?

The scripture does not say specifically, but Hannah probably rejoiced with Peninah, the other wife of their husband, Elkanah, when Peninah found out she was pregnant with their first child. Hannah probably celebrated with and supported her because she believed that soon she also would be with child. Child after child, she probably found herself congratulating Peninah on giving birth again and again.

But deep down, Hannah's heart was broken. Hannah wanted to have her own child. Not only did she have a broken heart, but Peninah's attitude toward Hannah changed. Peninah became prideful because she gave their husband what Hannah could not. So, she taunted and mocked Hannah. Have you been there? Have you celebrated others' successes and answered prayers only for them to turn around and ridicule you because you are still waiting?

Can you remember celebrating with your sister friends laughing, hugging one another, and being so happy and proud of their accomplishments and victories? But, when the celebration was over and you started driving home, you looked into your rearview mirror and saw the smile on your face fade as you heard a voice within you say, "You've been waiting and praying, and you still haven't gotten what you want."

You quickly rebuke the thought because it came across as if you were envious of your sister friend. In fact, it was just the opposite because you were genuinely happy for her. You just want what you want also. So, you whisper, "Lord, when will it be my turn?" You get home and the house is dark. You don't turn on any lights, but walk to the sofa, place your keys on the end table, and sit down as the tears begin to fall.

DISGUISING THE PAIN

Suddenly, the phone rings. One of your sister friends just called to make sure you made it home safely. As you talk, you hear the chatter in the background. Then you heard your name mentioned followed by, "She's been praying every day for ten years, going to church, trying to live that holy life, and where has it gotten her?"

Your sister friend hoped that you did not hear the conversation and briefly puts you on hold as she told the others that you were on the phone. But you did hear them, and yet you tell yourself that they would never know you heard those hurtful words. So, you acted like everything was okay. Immediately, you switched into your fake-happy voice and let her know that you made it home safely and that you really enjoyed yourself.

Despite the ridicule or whispers, will you continue to pray for what you want because you trust and believe God? What drives a person to continue in prayer day and night, month after month, year after year for the thing that they desire so deeply? Hannah, almost like a mad woman, refused to relinquish her desire of wanting something that, at the time, seemed unattainable.

BITTERNESS & DEPRESSION

The Scripture does not mention it, but after years of hoping and waiting, Hannah probably became depressed. The Bible states, she experienced "bitterness of soul."[1] In fact, she even, "stopped eating."[2] There weren't medications to ease her pain back then, but the Bible does state that her husband did do everything he could to comfort her, "Why eatest thou not? and why is thy heart grieved? Am not I better to thee than ten sons?"[3] Nothing Elkanah did helped to heal Hannah's broken heart or take away her desire to become a mother. Depression is often experienced by those who have been hoping for so long, even Christians.

Hannah had to endure taunting from inside her own home. Peninah, "her adversary, also provoked her sore and made her fret."[4] No matter how great the taunting was, it still did not diminish Hannah's desire for a child of her own.

WHY DID HANNAH KEEP HOPING?

Could it be because she had some knowledge about the God of Israel and what He could do? Stories passed from one generation to the next told how He brought the children of Israel out of Egypt and slew the Egyptian army. She heard about the plagues He caused to come upon the Egyptians because Pharaoh would not let the children of Israel go. She even heard about the miracles of manna and quail that the Lord provided as nourishment for the children of Israel in the wilderness after they fled Egypt. Was it the testimonies about the Lord that kept Hannah believing that she would get her heart's desire one day? Have you seen or heard some things about God that keep you believing?

When you have been praying about a certain thing for any length of time and have not heard anything from God, you can feel frustrated and even discouraged. How many times have you lifted your hands in praise and worship and made a declaration that in spite of the delay, you choose to believe God for the thing that you want? How many times have ministers pointed you out in church and said, "God said it would happen" but it's been years and you are still waiting? Why are you still holding on? Why do you want what you want? Let's see if we can delve deeper into Hannah's relentless desire to have a child. Then we may get answers to why we want some of the things we want.

CITIZENS OF GOD'S KINGDOM

Christians are citizens of God's kingdom. In a kingdom, the king dictates what goes on within his kingdom. "For God is the King of all the earth...."[5] Therefore, God already knew before we ever existed what He wanted accomplished in the earth. God delivered Israel many times, but they kept falling back and disregarding God's laws. So, whenever God wanted to get Israel's attention about breaking their covenant with Him, He would raise up a prophet.

In 1 Samuel 1, we mentioned earlier about Hannah wanting a child, but we did not mention why she could not have a child. So, what was the reason? "…The LORD had shut up her womb."[6] But she still wanted a child. Did Hannah want a child just to shut the mouths of the naysayers? Or, to prove that she was just as much of a woman as Peninah? Perhaps, she wanted to parade the child around for others to admire. Why was her desire to have a child so relentless?

THE LOOK OF SUCCESS

Whether it's academic accomplishments, marriage, high-level job and income, expensive stuff, millions in the bank, travelling around the world, or rubbing noses with the elite, why do we want what we want? Society has a way of defining success. We have embraced what it says a successful person looks like with open arms. Just like in Hannah's day, if a married woman does not have children, she may be looked down upon. According to society, a woman's primary purpose is to have children.

If we have not obtained a certain socio-economic status by a certain age, we are considered unsuccessful. Family members may suggest to us that we are getting older, and still have not done this or obtained that. They don't even realize that the very thing they are criticizing you for not having might be the very thing you've wanted and prayed about for years.

Perhaps, we desire certain things because we want to impress others. Maybe we want to prove our worth to someone that said we would never be anyone of prominence or have anything of value. There is absolutely nothing wrong with wanting nice things and trying to better ourselves. But do we ever really ask the Lord what we should want or, more importantly, "Lord, what do you want *for* me?"

Typically, when the "want" does not leave you, (as long as the "want" is not contrary to the Word of the Lord), we assume that God has placed the desire in our heart for a reason. This may or may not be the case. Sometimes our desires can be so intense that we can mistake the cries of our heart for the voice of God.

WHERE TO START

The best starting place is to simply ask God what His desires are for our lives. We're no longer asking God to jump on the bandwagon of our well thought out pursuits regardless of how noble they may be. Instead, our joy is rooted in Jesus. He becomes our greatest want. Then every other desire flows from the deepest longing we have for the Lord, Himself.

However, we see that Hannah's desire to have a baby was a burden God placed on her heart for His purpose. So, why did God shut her womb if this was all part of His plan? In 1 Samuel 1, it does not state that Hannah consistently prayed for a child. However, it does state that she desired a child year after year. One day, the burden of desiring a child and being taunted by Peninah became so great that Hannah left home and went to church to pray.

> "And she vowed a vow, and said, O Lord of hosts, if thou wilt indeed look on the affliction of thine handmaid, and remember me, and not forget thine handmaid, but wilt give unto thine handmaid a man child, then I will give him unto the Lord all the days of his life..." I Samuel 1:11a KJV

What changed? What caused Hannah to now go to the house of God to pray for a child? And not just any child, she wanted a boy. She even made a vow to God that if He granted her petition, she would give the child back to Him. We can't be mad at her for being specific. Most of us have been taught to pray this way. For years, we desire something so much, we pray over and over, asking God and telling Him, "If you give me what I want, I promise I will give it back to you."

I don't believe God answered Hannah's prayer because she bargained with Him. First, I think God answered her prayer because she finally asked Him. I don't recall anywhere before this that Hannah actually talked to the Lord about this. Second, it's quite possible that God answered Hannah's prayer because He was revealing a better way to pray. Instead of saying, God, if you give me what I want, I will give it back to you", God shows Hannah and us, that if we give Him what He wants, He will turn around and give back to us.

Remember, Israel was in a time of rebellion and disobedience. God wanted to get their attention. His divine plan was to have Hannah bear a prophet to tell Israel what He wanted them to know. When Hannah stopped wanting a child just for the sake of having a child and aligned her will with the will and purpose of the Lord, He granted her petition. "Elkanah knew Hannah his wife; and the Lord remembered her.[7]"

In the next chapter, we see God gave Hannah more children because it was no longer about what Hannah wanted. It was now about God's purpose being fulfilled in the earth. He needed the prophet, Samuel, to be birthed and to be His voice unto Israel.

FULFILLING HER PROMISE & HIS PURPOSE

When the time came, Hannah took Samuel to be raised in the house of the Lord by Eli, the priest, as she promised. Samuel had a great task ahead of him and he had to have an unshakable relationship with God. Eli was the one appointed at that time to teach Samuel about hearing and knowing the voice of God. Hannah had never before heard God's voice. Her connection to the Lord was through Eli. In fact, Eli was appointed by God as the priest over Israel as well as the mediator between God and Israel. So, when Hannah went to the temple to pray, it was Eli who told her that she would have her petition.

When you have a desire that seems to go unfulfilled, it just may be the Lord allowing you to understand what it's like when He's unable to get what He wants from humanity. Once we can understand God's perspective, we're better able to align our prayers with something He wants accomplished in the earth.

In the beginning, you may get weary. People may talk about you. You may even become discouraged. Stay the course, and do "not be weary in well doing: for in due season we shall reap, if we faint not."[8] Fall to your knees and tell the Lord, "This must be what You feel like when dealing with mankind. Forgive me, Lord. Tell me what You want." Remember, the Lord wanted a prophet. And after giving birth to Samuel, "The Lord visited Hannah, so that she conceived, and bore three sons and two daughters."[9] Hannah no longer hung her head low because her heart was made glad.

It may seem like the years of agony and waiting have taken their toll on you, and you may feel like what you want will never come to pass. You may be tired and even feel like giving up. You may even tell yourself that perhaps it is not God's will for you to have what you want. Family and friends may laugh at you and say you are wasting your life believing for something you haven't received in ten years. Don't be dismayed. Be like the woman who worried the unjust judge until he gave her what she wanted. (See Luke 18:6.) Be like the woman who would not give up hope of having her daughter delivered. Even though she knew that her people were considered as 'dogs' in the eyes of the Jews. (See Mark 7:27-29)

Although at one time Hannah's heart was broken, it was made glad by the Lord. "A merry heart doeth good like a medicine.[10]" Don't stop praying, trusting, hoping and believing. Just remember this, the next time you cry because of delayed blessings, stop and say, "Lord, this must be how You feel when I take my time responding. Forgive me. Now tell me, what do You want?" When you give God what He wants, He will give you the desires of your heart.

My name is Sandra Sledge,
and I am a JESUS Girl.

Sandra L. Sledge is an entrepreneur who loves and lives for the Lord Jesus Christ. She is a life- long resident of the state of Illinois. Saved and baptized in the Holy Spirit at an early age, Sandra shares the love of Jesus Christ and adamantly encourages others to give Him a try. Today, Sandra's desire is to see people free from the bondage of sin and living for the Lord Jesus Christ. She continues to spread the love and gospel with a genuine smile on her face and in her heart because she is so grateful that the LORD has chosen to use her "for such a time as this.".

CHAPTER 3

Abigail

A TIMELY RESPONSE

ABIGAIL TELLS HER STORY

(In Biblical Fiction Style)

> *Hello, my good people. My name is Abigail of Carmel, and I am what some may refer to as a Jesus Girl – someone who rises up and unexpectedly gives grace when she surely could have done otherwise. Someone who reveals the power, strength and mystery of Christ at work in her life and in the world! Simply put… "God is within her; she will not fall" (Psalm 46:5a NIV).*
>
> *I cannot believe this is my life. I find myself married to the wealthiest man in town named Nabal. Financially, I lack no good thing, but I feel my husband's love of money just*

might be the thing that causes our demise. I do not make that statement without merit. You see, my husband uses money in the most despicable ways, and he shamelessly flaunts his affluence around the region in which we live. He is a descendant of Caleb, from the tribe of Judah, but he loves money more than he loves God. That right there is a formula for disaster. He never uses good judgement and regularly offends anyone who even mildly opposes him. I tell you the truth: my husband is a fool!

Every time I turn around, I am making concessions for his rude, disrespectful, and evil dealings toward others. I often cry out to the Lord, "Father, how much longer must I endure this toxic relationship? I have always trusted You to lead, guide, and direct me in the ways I should go, and I do not intend to decide now without Your prompting me. However, my Lord, I still wonder about this perfect plan You have for my life because it's not quite what I imagined it to be!"

On the surface, my life appears to be the model for marital bliss. But, if the curtain were ever pulled back to expose the reality of our marriage, you would clearly see storms brewing. I know the day is coming when my husband will cross the wrong person, and death will come knocking at our door. How quickly God enables me to respond just may dictate life or death for me, my entire household, and a future king. I must always choose my words wisely and act with discretion. After all, my decisions could impact many lives and, possibly, cost me my own. "And if I perish, I perish." (See Esther 4:16b NIV)

So, what do you do when you are married to a fool, yet you are destined to marry a king? This was Abigail's dilemma and from her life journey, we may find principles that unlock answers to life as a Jesus Girl.

In 1 Samuel 25, we find Abigail married to Nabal. She is a wife, servant, mediator, protector, peacemaker, risk-taker, and intercessor. Although she is beautiful in appearance, it is her character, courage to move forward fearlessly in God, and her timely words of wisdom that cause her to stand out and shine.

Abigail does not get as much mention in the Bible as some of the other women, but that doesn't reduce her importance. Like Jesus, she lived most of her life in obscurity. You may be wondering how and why did this Jesus Girl end up marrying a man like Nabal? In the time this story was written, most marriages were arranged. It is likely that her parents selected him because of his wealth and status. Regardless, the fact remains that her character held up even with a difficult relationship in a loveless marriage.

What do you do when you are in a hard place? What is your response when you are faced with adversity? Will you murmur and complain or will you right the wrongs of others to bring peace, even if you are not to blame? The latter answer is, indeed, the Jesus Girl way!

CHARACTER TRAITS OF A JESUS GIRL

Let's take a look at Abigail's life and take note of some valuable character traits. Abigail consistently put others before herself. She was kind, humble, loyal and faithful in word and deed. The presence of God was always with her and fighting for her. She knew she was never alone. When you know that God is for you, then you simply do not consider who can be against you. When you trust God, your "nevertheless" comes quickly, and you are willing to go the distance with Him. That alone set her faith on fire and made her a force to be reckoned with!

Have you ever done what God told you to do and landed in a bad spot? If so, then you are in good company. Abigail's decision to follow God's plan instead of her own put her in harm's way. What started out as a normal day quickly changed when, without warning, Abigail received news from one of her servants that her husband had once again allowed his ignorance to disrespect a humble request from David, the future king. David was furious that Nabal so blatantly denied his request for food for his men after the years he spent protecting Nabal's wealth. In a rage of anger, David vowed to kill Nabal and his entire household. So, David gathered 400 of his men and were on their way to carry out those plans.

With no time to waste, Abigail had to decide quickly. Would she flee and save her own life (seeing this as a possible escape out of a bad marriage), or would she try to intercept David before he reached her home? What would you do? Be honest. What was your first thought? My first thought would have been like Forrest Gump, "Run Forrest, run!" I would have run away and never looked back.[1] But, if I were in Abigail's shoes and made a hasty escape, I would have missed my appointed time with destiny.

DESTINY DECISION

That one selfish decision could have caused many innocent lives to be lost. And what about David, God's choice for future king? Would he have missed his appointed time with destiny because Abigail was not in place to give wise counsel concerning a matter?

God's plans will never look like your plans because they involve more than just you. They will lead you on a journey to test your faith and surrender your will so that His will is done, and He will be glorified! God's plans are so much bigger than you and I.

So which road did Abigail choose? This Jesus Girl made a timely decision to intercept David before he reached her home. She had to act quickly, so she sent her servant ahead while she gathered up the food from their immense storehouse to meet David's original request. Abigail followed behind with food to feed his entire army of 600 men.

David was impressed by Abigail's discernment and humbleness. Her soft-spoken words put an end to David's anger, and he released great favor, peace and blessings upon her. Even today, Abigail's character reflects the life she lived before men and God.

Abigail was loyal. It is clear that this Jesus Girl was a loyal wife, servant and friend. The word "loyal" means giving or showing firm and constant support or allegiance to a person or institution.[2] We read in 1 Samuel 25:14-17 that the servants came to her to tell of the impending doom because of her husband's reckless behavior. Who better to know how you would respond than the servants? They knew she would do the right thing in spite of the circumstances.

Though she was not the happiest wife, she did not leave her husband. Even when she heard of this problem, she sought to protect her husband. For better or worse, she upheld her vow to Nabal. She also was loyal to David when she attempted to undo the damage her husband's hateful, unkind words nearly caused. Her willingness to provide nourishment for David physically and spiritually can be seen in verses 18, 27, and 32.

Lastly, she was loyal to God. At every turn, Abigail chose to trust God with her life. She was a demonstration of faith in God. He saw her heart and moved on her behalf. What about you...where does your loyalty lie?

Abigail was full of wisdom. Wisdom is the quality of having experience, knowledge, and good judgment...the quality of being wise.[3] When the servant told Abigail, that disaster was hanging over his master and household, her wisdom prevailed. Only wisdom could keep her strong while facing the matter before her. She wisely honored David's request for food for his men and bypassed her husband, knowing he would either delay or even forbid her actions.

She also exhibited wisdom when she bowed down in submission to David. Finally, in verse 41 and 42, after Nabal was dead, David sent word to Abigail, asking her to become his wife. Wisdom prevailed yet again when she bowed down before his servants to give her response and then quickly got on a donkey to meet her king indicating she was ready to serve David as "his" wife. Are you full of wisdom?

Abigail was a peacemaker. A peacemaker is defined as a person who brings about peace by reconciling adversaries, like a mediator or an intercessor.[4] They are friendly, agreeable, adaptable, trusting, and easy going. Abigail apologized for her husband's rude behavior and took the blame for not fulfilling David's request. In verse 26, Abigail reminded David of his covenant with God and that he need not shed innocent blood out of anger because God would fight his enemies. Then, in verses 32 and 33, David thanked God for sending Abigail to meet him, and, most importantly, he blessed her for using good judgment. Are you a peacemaker?

Abigail vowed to always protect her husband's interests at all costs, even when he was lacking in judgment and character. Her timely response to speak wisdom and truth into David's life stopped him from making a rash decision. She constantly denied herself for the sake of others. What has Abigail's life taught you?

WHEN LIFE DOESN'T LOOK LIKE YOU THOUGHT IT WOULD?

Like Abigail, I, too, thought my life would look quite different than it does today. I sometimes find myself wondering how God is going to use the rest of my life in His glorious plan. I imagined by now, I would be living my best life at 51, happily married to my king and enjoying our kids and grandkids. Financially, we would be lacking no good thing as we funded kingdom projects through our multiple prosperous enterprises. God's dynamic duo would be traveling the world teaching the Word of God and making disciples as we reveal the love of Jesus to a hurting and dying world. That's how I envisioned life to be, but that is not yet my reality. Nevertheless, I choose to follow Abigail's example to trust God's plan and be willing to go the distance with Him. I thank God for the glimpses of greatness He continues to show me on this life journey.

God is moving and building my character, one step at a time and I am reminded to never despise the day of humble beginnings. What was once a hobby, has slowly turned into a small business that will one day flourish into a prosperous enterprise. What God has promised will surely come to pass. This Jesus Girl believes that by this time next year, we (me and my king) will be happily married, enjoying family and funding kingdom projects. Also, in the past two years, ministry outreach and travel has begun to increase because doors for speaking engagements are coming forth. My God-ordained assignment to lead a weekly conference line Bible study has now expanded to Facebook live. My steps have been ordered by God and if I manage the little He has given me with faithfulness and integrity, He will trust me with greater responsibilities. Just as Abigail trusted God with her life plans, so will I.

God has been faithful throughout my journey. When I look back over my life, I see now that, when I walked away from the house, car, job, friends and family to follow Jesus, none of that was in vain. Many people thought I was crazy because they could not believe that God would do something so drastic. But Jesus made that same drastic decision to leave everything in heaven to come and save humanity. It has prepared me to look at things from an eternal perspective and not a temporal one. Nothing compares to knowing Jesus intimately and hearing His still small voice.

This peace that I have… the world didn't give it to me, and the world cannot take it away. So, what do you do when life looks contrary to God's Word? Trust Him and remember what He told you in the secret place because it still holds true today. Do not be moved by what you see or feel but by what God said. Act quickly on His word because your timely response doesn't just affect you but all those around you. If you have any doubt what He said, ask Him first and He will bring it back to your remembrance. I am confident God's plan is the best plan, and He is working behind the scenes to fulfill His promises to all His Jesus Girls!

My name is Sonya Ratcliff,
and I am a JESUS Girl.

Sonya Ratcliff is a multi-faceted woman of God with a heart for worship. She is an evangelist and ordained minister who serves in leadership at Destiny Generation Ministries Church in Dallas, TX. In addition, she is the founder of Love Without Limits Ministry and 4G International Mentorship, both non-profit ministries designed to teach, inspire, equip and encourage a life of purity and holiness while passionately pursuing a personal relationship with Christ Jesus. Her heart's desire is to make disciples who are healed and made whole through the Word and love of God. She is the proud mother of two beautiful children, Bria and Brandon, and one grandson, Kaleb.

CHAPTER 4

Esther

IN PREPARATION FOR THE KING & YOUR PURPOSE

Prepared: made ready for use[1], subjected to a special process or treatment.[2] Merriam-Webster

PREPARING FOR THE KING

The woman I want to look at from the Bible is Esther. Esther was adopted by her cousin Mordecai after the loss of her parents. She was beautiful of form and face, so her outer appearance attracted many. She was smart, well-mannered, a great listener and obedient. What a description! At that time, the king was in search of a new bride and all the young, beautiful virgins were ordered to appear and audition for him.

Let's look at part of her story:

"When the king's order and edict had been proclaimed, many young women were brought to the citadel of Susa and put under the care of Hagai. Esther also was taken to the king's palace and entrusted to Hagai, who had charge of the harem. She pleased him and won his favor. Immediately he provided her with her beauty treatments and special food. He assigned to her seven female attendants selected from the king's palace and moved her and her attendants into the best place in the harem." (Esther 2:8-9 NIV)

"Before a young woman's turn came to go into King Xerxes, she had to complete twelve months of beauty treatments prescribed for the women, six months with oil of myrrh and six with perfumes and cosmetics." (Esther 2:12 NIV)

So, Esther and the other 'contestants' were given one year of preparation after which they were called by name to come before the king. And what a year it was. Can you imagine six months of oil of myrrh treatments and six months of perfumes and cosmetic treatments? This was the ultimate in skin, beauty and day spa therapy. And yet after all of that, there was only one woman chosen.

"Now the king was attracted to Esther more than to any of the other women, and she won his favor and approval more than any of the other virgins. So, he set a royal crown on her head and made her queen instead of Vashti." (Esther 2:17 NIV)

I think about the preparation process and what it takes to get ready from a natural standpoint, if you take time to prepare yourself. Let's be honest I know many women don't put much preparation into getting themselves spiritually prepared, but the physical preparation takes all our time. We may go to the extreme in finding ways to make our outer selves look amazing.

As I read her story fully, I realized not only did she find favor with Hagai, she found favor with the king. This led me to believe that her obedience with all the requirements put in place prepared her for her visit with the King. She was faithful to the process of her preparation.

This was an eye-opener for me. How unprepared most of us are spiritually speaking. If you were selected to meet the King, would you be prepared?

Seriously, consider the amount of time it took to groom oneself to just be in the presence of the king. Do you hear me? To be allowed into the presence of the king required an *entire year* of perfumed baths. After all that work, you still might not be the chosen one. Unfortunately, it seems like a bit much, but remember getting prepared requires thought and time. After you have been stripped of the old, the preparation process is quite extensive because it involves every area of your life.

PREPARATION REQUIRES PURSUING CHRIST

The preparation process starts with a spiritual mindset which requires us to be in pursuit of Christ. This pursuit requires us to be surrendered, totally surrendered and intimate with our King Jesus. There is no possible way to be committed, faithful and walk in obedience with man unless we first do so with our Father.

I had to be broke and broken before I could understand the reality of what pursuing Christ really meant. I had sacrificed so much to do things the world's way that I honestly didn't even consider the spiritual side of life.

I was raised going to church, singing in the choir, serving on the usher board, and going to Baptist Training Union. With all that, I never knew that all He required was a relationship. So much focus is put on the religious side of this that often the relationship portion is not taught. The truth is, after participation in all those required programs, I walked away not knowing anything more than a program. No real relationship was ever established. Finally, I learned intimacy with Christ placed me in a position to abide in spiritual obedience, favor and preparation to meet the King.

Pursuing Christ must be a priority over pursuing man. The pursuit of Christ has great rewards with no disappointments. That's not to say there won't be trials. Remember, we have not always chosen the path of righteousness. Our journey, or at least my journey, has been about what I wanted more so than what He desired for me. My pursuit for the world's way left me so unprepared for *THE* King!

PREPARING FOR YOUR PURPOSE

Later in Esther's story, we read that Haman, one of the king's key advisors, manipulates the king into ordering all Jews to be killed. As of that time,

> "Esther had not revealed her nationality and family background, because Mordecai had forbidden her to do so." Esther 2:10 NIV

She and her family were Jews, and if found out, they would be subject to the king's order. Here she was living in the palace as queen, yet her life and the lives of her people were now in grave danger. Mordecai suggested she use her position with the king to persuade him to change his mind and save her people. This action would mean literally putting her life on the line.

(Esther sent this message to her cousin Mordecai.) "All the king's officials and the people of the royal provinces know that for any man or woman who approaches the king in the inner court without being summoned the king has but one law: that they be put to death unless the king extends the gold scepter to them and spares their lives. But thirty days have passed since I was called to go to the king." Esther 4:11 NIV

She was unsure where she stood with the king because it had been a month since he called for her.

"When Esther's words were reported to Mordecai, he sent back this answer: 'Do not think that because you are in the king's house you alone of all the Jews will escape. For if you remain silent at this time, relief and deliverance for the Jews will arise from another place, but you and your father's family will perish. And who knows but that you have come to your royal position for such a time as this?'" (Esther 4:12-14 NIV)

She was in a position of favor with the king, but still had to risk her life to stand up and save her people. While she alone had to be the one to walk into the king's presence, she wanted her people to join her as she prepared herself for that assignment.

"Then Esther sent this reply to Mordecai: 'Go, gather together all the Jews who are in Susa, and fast for me. Do not eat or drink for three days, night or day. I and my attendants will fast as you do. When this is done, I will go to the king, even though it is against the law. And if I perish, I perish.'" (Esther 4:15-16 NIV)

She was willing, in spiritual preparation, to go above and beyond even at the cost of her life. That was a price she was willing to pay. As I thought about her preparation for the greater purpose in which God was calling her to, it showed me that I was spiritually unprepared for what God had planned for my life.

> "You're hopeless, you religion scholars and Pharisees! Frauds! You're like manicured grave plots, grass clipped and the flowers bright, but six feet down it's all rotting bones and worm-eaten flesh. People look at you and think you're saints, but beneath the skin you're total frauds." (Matthew 23:27-28 MSG)

This is pretty much where I was with my own level of spiritual preparation. I appeared to be prepared on the outside, but I was messed-up on the inside. As I thought about being prepared, the natural things came to mind faster than the spiritual. I finally asked the Lord to show me what it was that He was requiring of me.

Of course, I know it's the spiritual side that He delights in, but I had been so consumed with the natural side that I hadn't considered the neglect of my spiritual preparedness. There have been times in my life where I needed to draw upon the preparation, and it wasn't there. I wasn't ready. Maybe you can relate? If your purpose, your dream knocked on your door, would you be ready? I know you would be excited, but would you be prepared?

Esther is a prime example of preparing for and walking out God's plan and purpose for her life. Just like in Jeremiah 29:11, God knew the plans He had for Esther, even before she was formed in the womb.

The thought of walking out the plans God has destined for me births pure excitement and I really desire to do just that. The key word here is desire. I have moved past worrying so much about programs, rituals and human expectations. I choose to ask God how I can prepare for the next season of my life.

When it is all said and done, does your preparation include your inner, spiritual self as well? Are you willing to do what it takes to prepare for the King and His purpose for your life? Are you able to hear His voice directing you where to go, when to stand up for something or when to humbly wait for Him to summon you?

With every ounce of her courage and preparation, Esther went before her husband, the king, to plead for the lives of her people. She found favor in his eyes and garnered this level of loyalty and protection for the Jews:

> "The king's edict granted the Jews in every city the right to assemble and protect themselves; to destroy, kill and annihilate the armed men of any nationality or province who might attack them and their women and children, and to plunder the property of their enemies." (Esther 8:11 NIV)

My name is Myrtle Carter,
and I am a JESUS Girl.

Myrtle Carter is a child of God and business owner whose passion is to understand God's Word and walk in the calling He has on her life. As a prayer warrior, she intercedes on behalf of those that need prayer. She is the mother of two daughters and one son, and the grandmother of seven grandsons and two granddaughters. Myrtle uses her God-given creativity as an event designer and is member of Central Church of Manor, Texas.

CHAPTER 5

Gomer

CHANGING POSITIONS

MOST REBELLIOUS

Have you ever heard the phrase "like mother like daughter"? This saying typically means "when a daughter takes after her mother in terms of mannerism, interest, behavior, etc." I can say that I'm like my mother in more ways than I like to admit. My mother has always been a hard-working woman with much endurance. She's loving, nurturing and able to make something out of little. If I let my husband tell his story, he'd say I get the fussing from my mother too. However, if the truth were told, I am my fathers' daughter also. Like my father, I am determined to not allow anything stop me from what I want or what I believe in.

In the early 90's, just a year after high school, I found myself a stripper in a strip club, first in Atlanta, Ga, then in Miami, Fl. During my five years of pole dancing, I encountered so many young women. Many of the women were looking for their fathers in relationships. Others had suffered from some form of abuse, such as rape, molestation, physical/verbal abuse, or drug/alcohol abuse. Their abuse had led them to the strip club. For me, it was pure rebellion.

Yes, if there was an award for the most rebellious child, it would have been mine. Most of the women were looking for love in all the wrong places. How many of us do that? For some, the wrong place may have been a relationship, drugs, alcohol, material things, gaining status or fame, or even settling for some baller, pimp, or even other women.

Some of these young girls, starting at age 14, (yes. I said 14) became strippers because they were just looking for the family they never had. I met ladies that started off as students paying their way through college as strippers, but later became career strippers. Some of them went to school and became nurses yet decided to remain as strippers because they made more money. I have numerous stories of young ladies whose intentions were to dance for only a few months. Those months turned into years and years, with some resulting in death from suicide, drug or alcohol abuse, physical abuse, or even H.I.V. and AIDS. Of course, there were also many turn-around stories, mine being one them, all because of the blood of Jesus Christ.

GENERATIONAL OPPRESSION

In the book of Hosea, God reveals the story of Gomer – another 'lady of the night' and daughter of Diblaim. Like Gomer, Diblaim was a prostitute...again like mother, like daughter.[1] Some say prostitution is the oldest profession in the world, but I say it's the oldest oppression. The enemy uses prostitution to keep women in generational bondage. There have been many times where I've seen generational patterns. Every woman within the family unit were divorced or never married, from the grandmother all the way down to the great granddaughters. I have seen the same ongoing oppression from generation to generation even when the person didn't have a chance to know their ancestors. It's in the bloodline.

Gomer may have thought, 'I will not be like my mama,' but found herself being just like her anyway. I'm sure it wasn't Gomer's dream to grow up and become a prostitute. Sometimes the very thing we despise, we become.

MARRY A PROSTITUTE?

As the story goes, Hosea, a prophet, hears the audible voice of God for the first time. He had to be surprised and probably shocked when God told him to marry a prostitute and have children of whoredom. Ok, now wait a minute, what?! The Lord said to him, *"Go, marry a promiscuous woman and have children with her, for like an adulterous wife this land is guilty of unfaithfulness to the Lord."* (Hosea 1:2b NIV)

Gomer was a woman of whoredom, a promiscuous woman, and a prostitute. Can you imagine Gomer's surprise that a Prophet of God would want to marry her and make a whore into a housewife? I can imagine Gomer may have felt as though she was being pranked.

Why would an upright man of God take her as a wife? Maybe she had some mixed emotions believing she could become a wholesome housewife. Maybe she just felt excited to get out of the streets and finally get some appropriate affection. Hosea and Gomer had nothing in common. While Hosea was serving the people, Gomer was serving the men in the neighborhood.

NAMES HAVE POWER

Hosea and Gomer were married and together had three children, Jezreel (God sows), Lo-Ruhamah (which means "not loved"), and Lo-Ammi (which means "not my people").[2]

Names have power. Even though Gomer had been known as the prostitute, Gomer's name meant "complete finish or completion."[3] This is how God saw her – complete and finished. He also sees our story this way even when we have been disobedient or full of procrastination. This is a reminder of the unconditional love Christ has for us. He knows all about us and yet He still loves us!

For many years as a stripper, I had a stage name. I wouldn't share my birth name because I didn't like it. One day, I found out my name, Nia, means "purpose." I now know why Satan did not want me to be comfortable with or even like my name. I am purpose, and I have purpose!

KNOW YOUR WORTH

Do you know that God loves us so much, *"that he gave his one and only Son, that whoever believes in him shall not perish but have eternal life."*[4] He made the ultimate sacrifice. What He did for us was something that we wouldn't have done for anyone. I have two children, a boy and a girl, I know I would never give either one of them up for anyone else.

God sees us from the beginning. Jeremiah 1:5 (NLT) says *"I knew you before I formed you in your mother's womb."* God loves us despite anything we do or say. We are valuable to Christ. Many of us don't know who we really are so we settle for less and allow people to treat us any way they choose. God says we are a royal priesthood, a called-out nation. We are His people and He is our Father. Whatever belongs to Daddy, belongs to us. (See 1 Peter 2:9.)

YOU ARE NOT YOUR OWN

Do you know your body is not your own? 1 Corinthians 6:19 (NIV) says, *"Do you not know that your bodies are temples of the Holy Spirit, who is in you, whom you have received from God? You are not your own;"*. We all must present our bodies as a living sacrifice, holy and acceptable to Him. We belong to God and must allow Him to be Lord.

There are men and women who have gotten distracted. Peter became distracted by the wind and waves when he was walking on the water to Jesus. Samson got distracted by Delilah's curves and beauty. What or who has your attention? Events? Career? Social media? Your destiny? I am guilty, too. One night, I set some time aside to spend with God and I picked up my phone to get to my Bible app. An hour later, I had no idea how I ended up on Social Media. I realized how easy God's time was stolen or should I say given away by distraction.

How do you feel after eating food that looked good yet left you feeling like you wasted your money, time and dining experience? Well, that's how I felt after being on social media for an hour. I felt irritated, unfulfilled and frustrated that I didn't give God His time. Romans 12:2a (NIV) says, *"Do not conform to the pattern of this world, but be transformed by the renewing of your mind."*

PURCHASED BACK – FORGIVEN

Hosea is told to reconcile with his wife. *"So I bought her for fifteen shekels of silver and about a homer and a lethek of barley. Then I told her, 'You are to live with me many days; you must not be a prostitute or be intimate with any man, and I will behave the same way toward you.'"* (Hosea 3:2-3 NIV)

If you look at what he paid to purchase Gomer, versus the normal going rate of that time, you will realize she was bought on sale. Sometimes, as women, we devalue or cheapen ourselves for less than the best, including settling for the in-the-meantime, in-between-time guy. We should learn to wait on God's best and trust that God only gives good gifts. We need to know who we belong to and become like the one we belong to, Jesus Christ.

Now, we see in the story that Gomer kept going to other lovers. From the looks of it, she had been back and forth for a long period of time. The kid's names spoke for themselves, hinting that some were probably not Hosea's children. His patience was most likely wearing thin considering that the children he claimed may have been children of whoredom. He also probably felt angry and embarrassed about his wife, just as God felt about Israel.

At one point we see Hosea even talking to one of the kids about their momma. How do you act when things aren't going your way or when you're betrayed, hurt, and embarrassed by the people you love? I can imagine how difficult this was for Hosea. I wonder at times if he had doubts? Maybe he asked, "Lord did you even say this? It's been awhile and I have had to endure so many trials, tribulations and foolishness. It looks like what you said isn't true."

Have you ever felt like that? Maybe it's been years and you have given up hope believing something will happen. But we need to trust God and His Word. God will perform His Word. He is a promise keeper. We are to trust Him even when it hurts, when it doesn't look good or feel good. You are to trust Him when you have three adulterous kids or a mother of prostitution. If you are feeling discouraged, the Bible says to wait on the Lord and He will renew your strength. (See Isaiah 40:31 TLB)

So, Hosea buys her back from the district market. The Bible doesn't specify why there was a cost, but it is interesting that he had to pay for her even though she already belonged to him by law. He had to pay to forgive the debt of her choices.

Did you know that God paid the ultimate price for us? We belonged to God, but because of our sin and walking away from Him, He paid to redeem us back to Himself. The Bible says that "For God so loved the world that He gave (as a price) His only begotten Son." For who? Us! It cost God everything. (See John 3:16)

WHORING AFTER OTHER GODS

God gave me a very difficult prophetic word to give to a beloved group of people. He told me to warn them. The Lord said, "Warning: put down your idol gods!" He said it twice, so I did as well. I began to cry at the thought of the warning because God does not give warnings and not mean it.

I can only imagine the weight on Hosea to bear the burden of warning an entire nation. God sent Hosea to Israel not only with a prophetic word, but through his own life as an example concerning their current state of offense. The message was "Repent!"

Between each child Gomer birthed to Hosea, she went out looking for her lovers and whoring after other gods. She believed that her myrrh, frankincense, the new moon, and sabbaths (pagan gods) were from her lovers. These were the same things Israel did to God. In Hosea 8, the Israelites took the gifts God gave them and built idol gods in the temple. The people of Israel had completely gotten away from trusting God.

God used a marriage to correlate a husband to represent God, and a wife to represent His people (Old Testament). In the New Testament, a husband represents Christ, and the wife represents the church. God wanted Israel to know that they were His bride.

Too often we have gone out whoring after other gods like relationships, careers, family, ministry and the list goes on. We can place everything and everyone before God. For example, God gives us a job or business and we keep all the money while not taking care of His house. Exodus 20:3 (NKJV) says, *"You shall have no other gods before Me."*

Ask yourself, who or what is your first priority? Is God first and foremost? Before your spouse or children? Before your wonderful job? Like Gomer and the Israelites, God wants us to return to Him. If God asks us to return, that means He never left.

PROSTITUTE TO PROSTRATE

Gomer changed positions. In the process of this change, did she go from laying on her back as a prostitute to laying on her face before the Lord, or just submission, or both? Gomer changed positions from prostitute to prostrate. I looked up "prostitution" in Merriam-Webster's dictionary. The definition reads, "the act or practice of engaging in promiscuous sexual relations especially for money".[5] After I read what it meant, the Lord told me to look down at the next word under prostitute, "prostrate." Webster's definition says, "stretched out with face on the ground in adoration or submission."

The Lord told me this is what Gomer did. Gomer changed position when she came home to her husband after he purchased her back. He wanted her to stay with him and she did. Chapter after chapter, God warns and pleads with Israel to return to Him. I remember when God told me about Gomer changing positions. I always thought it meant to lay face down to the Lord. But now, I also realize it means to have a heart of submission. *"For the Lord does not see as man sees; for man looks at the outward appearance, but the Lord looks at the heart."* (1 Samuel 16:7b.) God is after a heart that's willing to lay prostrate before Him.

When the Lord spoke those words to me, I quickly understood because I had had my Gomer experience.

MY TESTIMONY

One day, I was invited to church by a young lady at the strip club. She invited me one Sunday to go to her church but she never came back again. I continued to go each week. Every Sunday I kept the same routine. I would leave church, grab a bite to eat, take a nap and go to work at the club. One day, I had this deep conviction that I needed to stop stripping. I told the Lord, "I want to get out, but I don't want to be a broke ex-stripper."

Then something unexplainable happened. After months of attending church, I went to the strip club on my day off. It was Miami's Monday night boxing when the strippers got in the ring to box each other for money. I went straight to the bar and ordered a gin and lime. As I went to pick it up, I had an open vision where everything in the room slowed down and the music stopped. Everyone was moving in very slow motion like in the movie the Matrix where the actor falls backwards dodging the bullets that were being shot at him. I thought this kind of stuff only happened on TV. However, I was living out a sort of make believe, motion picture experience that was very real.

As I stood there observing the women as they held their arms suspended in mid-air while still moving at a snail's pace, there was complete silence. The DJ was scratching the record on his turntable, the people were all laughing and doing things that usually make noise but there was absolutely no sound to be heard. It was like somebody pressed the mute button in that moment. The only sound I heard was the voice of God saying, "This is hell. Do you want to stay?"

Immediately after the Lord spoke these words, the sound and movement all returned to normal at the same time. I know what you're thinking. What was she drinking? But the truth is I hadn't had anything yet. This was totally supernatural. And as soon as I put my drink down, the fear of the Lord fell on me. From my experience, I don't know of any drug or drink that can produce the fear of the Lord. That's how I know my experience was from God. Nothing like this had ever happened to me before. It was more real than what I had ever encountered in my life. I stayed the entire night but I was afraid.

What happened to me after that was even more extraordinary. The Lord prepared me for my exit. I transformed my garage into a beauty salon. The only time I went back to the club was to share the gospel with the women. Fast forward years later, many of the women that God snatched out of that club are now ministers, evangelists, motivational speakers, business owners, and most of all, they are Christians. But all of this started when God spoke to me and I obeyed.

It was only at His Word that I changed positions from being a hard-working stripper that loved money to a Jesus Girl that fell in love with the Lord. One day God spoke the Word over Gomer. I believe Gomer changed positions from being a prostitute to prostrate. Everything changed when the Lord spoke to me. Now I am one of the founding members and first lady of Christ For All Nations Church of Belleville IL, and also the visionary of the Jesus Girl!

My name is Nia Owens,
and I am a JESUS Girl.

Nia Owens, visionary of Jesus Girl, is an entrepreneur and founding member of Christ for all Nations Church. As a native of East St. Louis, Illinois, she launched a national morning prayer call over ten years ago called Sunday Morning Gravy. Nia helped pioneer How to Heal the Sick conferences along with her husband which has been instrumental in equipping and training disciples to operate in the supernatural and expand God's kingdom. She is the wife to Pastor Mike Owens and has two children, Gavin and Micah.

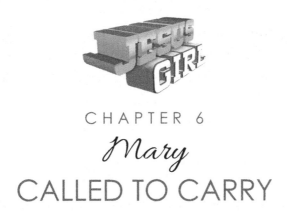

CHAPTER 6

Mary
CALLED TO CARRY

SEEING MY CALLING

At twenty-one years old, I met Jesus and fell madly in love...that is, after I crashed to the floor. I was a self-mutilating, drug-addicted lesbian who didn't believe in God. It was under His amazing power that I first-handedly experienced that God was really God. When I got up off the floor, my whole world was brand new. I was forgiven and clean in the blood of Jesus.

One month after my radical conversion, I experienced an open vision for the first time. I was in my friend's bedroom alone one night while worship music was playing. Suddenly, a section of the room began to fade to black. I blinked many times to clear my eyes, but the black screen remained. Suddenly, a silent movie clip began playing on the screen. I was standing on a massive outdoor stage at night with a microphone in my hand preaching to thousands of people. I witnessed the power of God moving through me for these people. Then, in an instant, the screen vanished and the wall in front of me reappeared. I was in such awe of what happened, I fell to my knees in worship.

What a holy moment of God as He showed me what He created me for. With a mixture of fear, intimidation, honor, and the 'ooey gooeys', I hold that vision close to my heart knowing one day I will see the manifestation of God's promise. In the ten years of what many call 'waiting' for this to happen, I've found that we are never really waiting, or at least we are not supposed to be. Waiting denotes standing still, an inactive position.

In the story of Mary, mother of Jesus, the Lord teaches us, start to finish, how to receive, carry, nurture, and birth His promises over our lifetime. Many of us get stuck at the receiving part, and others of us, at the carry and nurture part. Numerous saints have mountain-moving callings, but are misinformed on how to manage a successful "pregnancy". This results in too many premature births (underdeveloped ministries), late deliveries (missed appointments), and even abortions (rejection and abandonment of His calling).

To gain perspective on what answering the call God's way looks like, let's examine Mary's example:

> *"In the sixth month of Elizabeth's pregnancy, God sent the angel Gabriel to Nazareth, a town in Galilee, to a virgin pledged to be married to a man named Joseph, a descendant of David. The virgin's name was Mary. The angel went to her and said, "Greetings, you who are highly favored! The Lord is with you." Mary was greatly troubled at his words and wondered what kind of greeting this might be. But the angel said to her,*

"Do not be afraid, Mary; you have found favor with God. You will conceive and give birth to a son, and you are to call him Jesus. He will be great and will be called the Son of the Most High. The Lord God will give him the throne of his father David, and he will reign over Jacob's descendants forever; his kingdom will never end." "How will this be," Mary asked the angel, "since I am a virgin?" The angel answered, "The Holy Spirit will come on you, and the power of the Most High will overshadow you. So the holy one to be born will be called the Son of God. Even Elizabeth your relative is going to have a child in her old age, and she who was said to be unable to conceive is in her sixth month. For no word from God will ever fail." "I am the Lord's servant," Mary answered. "May your word to me be fulfilled." Then the angel left her." – (Luke 1:26-38 NIV)

What an incredible moment in history that would change lives for all eternity! Mary is often and rightfully praised for being called out by the Lord and giving birth to our beloved Jesus. But let's dig a little deeper into Mary's story, because it is her immediate response and how she walks out her journey that illustrates a life laid before the King.

WHAT WAS SO SPECIAL ABOUT MARY?

Mary, a young teenage girl from a small town, was likely living a simple life and was engaged to be married. On what was probably a normal day with friends, chores, family, and pondering what her future would be like as a married woman, God drops in. He calls her out from amongst her peers, family, and traditions to carry and birth the Son of God. The exact magnitude of this moment cannot be felt by any human on earth except Mary. Everything changes for her the moment she is called out by God. She can't go back to old ways, old plans, or old patterns of thinking. No longer will she only consider her wants and desires.

Another life within her has to come first in her decisions, choices, and considerations.

When reading this story, I often wonder what made Mary so special? She's not a princess, not educated, and there's no mention of her popularity or devotion in the temple. Her family isn't rich or exceptionally successful, and she didn't have the most life experience. She seems normal or ordinary. Nothing she is, could do, has done, thinks, believes, possesses, produces or performs made her "the one" for this calling. Yet, the first thing the angel said to Mary was *"you who are highly favored."*[1] You may have heard 1 Corinthians 1:27-29 (NIV) summarized as, "God doesn't call the qualified, but He qualifies those He called." This was exactly what the angel was saying when he declared God's favor over Mary.

Mary was simply favored by God! That's it! And like Mary, our calling has nothing to do with how special we or others think we are. It's not about how qualified we are, how hard we work, or how much we perform for God or others. It is all based on the Lord and His goodness falling upon us to do His holy will. He gives favor to whom He chooses. He chose me to write this book. He chose you to fulfill your calling! You are called because you are favored. This means nothing you possess, produce, are, could do, have done, think, believe, or perform made you "the one" for this calling. You're still chosen even if you stumble, fail, forget, fall off, or even reject it at first. He is not going to change His mind. So, you might as well walk in what He is asking you to do. Allow any doubt or worthlessness you may have felt to be released by that truth right there. Your past doesn't matter. Anything you lack doesn't matter.

In Exodus, when God calls Moses to deliver Israel out of Egypt, Moses gives God every excuse of why he shouldn't be chosen. He feels incapable, inadequate, and unusable. All of his fears and doubts are met with solutions God prepared in advance. Like Moses, God has already gone before you and solved every problem you can think of and empowered you with everything you'll need!

CARRIERS OF CHRIST

As you are reading this, some of you may say, "I don't even know what my calling is, so I don't know what you're talking about." Don't worry. You'll find out in about two minutes as you continue to read. Others of you are remembering that old church mother with the missing teeth prophesying to you about how God has called you out and telling you all He has destined for you. Ok, so maybe she wasn't missing her teeth.

Maybe it was your pastor or Christian friend who saw God's calling within you. Perhaps it was a guest preacher you never heard of who singled you out and laid hands on you. Maybe you had a Mary experience where it was just you and God. No matter what your called-out experience was, the point is you know you are called by God. You may not know we all share the exact same call as Mary. What?!

Don't freak out and rush for the pregnancy tests. We are not all going to give birth to the Lord Jesus, again (yikes!). But we are all called to carry Christ within us, spiritually. When we make Jesus Lord of our lives and are born again, the Holy Spirit makes His home inside of us. We become a temple, a carrier of God Himself (1 Corinthians 6:19). Like Mary, it's no longer ourselves we have to consider. Jesus living within us must come first in our decisions, choices, and considerations.

We are to possess the Holy Spirit within and bear the image of God without. This means that whether you know your specific individual calling or not, you know your universal calling. You are called to give birth to God's plans and purposes. Like Mary, you will deliver Jesus to others. Through you, the world will know that Jesus lives, He is the one true God, He loves them, and He paid a price to redeem them.

Through your carrying, you will reveal the true nature of the Father and be a witness to all the world that Jesus reigns!

There is no greater calling than this. Every purpose, plan, and prophecy God has revealed to you sum up into one thing, carry Christ. Were you prophesied to be a pastor? It means you are called to carry Christ. Did God give you a dream to build a homeless shelter? You're called to carry Christ. Did the Holy Spirit show you adopting kids from other countries? You're called to carry Christ. Are you sitting on the church pew every Sunday waiting to learn about your future? You're called to carry Christ. Whether you're on that pew, at your job, in your home, at the grocery store, or at your favorite nail shop, you are delivering Christ to those around you. There are no exceptions to this call. We have all been given a universal mandate from heaven to carry the Lord Jesus to the world.

The uniqueness of all our destinies are purposed by God through His sovereign will. We cannot boast in ourselves or compare it to someone else's. Our calling doesn't make us great. What makes us great is Him. Rejoice in the God of specific and divine design and be honored by the life He planned for you.

MARY'S DEFINING MOMENT

After the angel reveals to Mary what the Lord will do in her, Mary asks a simple, but powerful question, *"How will this be...since I am a virgin?"*[2] If I could insert an emoji face right here, it would definitely be the shocked face with one hand on each cheek with the jaw dropped wide open. *Why is this powerful*, you ask? Let's look at why she asked this question.

When I first read this story, I imagined myself in her shoes and thought, *if I'm already engaged to be married and an angel tells me that I'm going to conceive and bear God's child, then I would think 'Cool! When we get married, we're going to have a son named Jesus'.* Pretty straight forward, right?! But I would have been so very wrong. We have to be careful not to assume human understanding in God's supernatural plans.

Mary was asking God how He would fulfill His Word. She didn't take the word and try to figure out how she could make it happen, she asked how God was going to make it happen. Is it such a crazy thought to consider God has a specific plan to achieve His purpose? After the angel tells her how God is going to do this seemingly impossible thing, she says *"I am the Lord's servant, may your word to me be fulfilled."*[3] In faith, Mary offered herself to God as a willing vessel. It's what she had to give. She replied, "Yes" to her Lord when He called.

THE WEIGHT OF HER "YES"

To understand the significance of Mary's "yes", is to understand what was really asked of her. When the angel tells Mary she has found favor with God, I wonder if it felt like favor to her? Perhaps at the beginning, receiving a word like that would feel amazing. 'Yay God!' But then the magnitude of what was being asked of her becomes real.

Mary's "yes" led her to the edge of the unknown. She didn't know if she would be cut off from her family whom she depended on or discarded by her fiancé. Would she become homeless, helpless, and void of all the security and provision she had as a young girl? That's a big risk! Being asked to give birth wasn't one simple solitary act. She was also being asked to be set apart from the world and still remain holy.

She was asked to endure persecution, slander, mistreatment, disownment, lies and scorn. She was going to endure a lot of physical, mental, and emotional pain because of her obedience. Her will would be tested constantly. Answering "yes" meant she wasn't able to live like all the other girls in her village or have the fairytale life she dreamed of. She had to place her own ambitions and ways aside for the King. From the moment she said "yes", it was about God's will and His way.

Mary wasn't super-human. Since the Bible doesn't mention her emotional state throughout this journey, we often assume that she didn't have a problem or that she was just perfect in keeping it all together and in perspective. But I don't think she did. She was likely scared, lonely in the weight of the call, made fun of, hurt, sad at times, intimidated, and shamed in front of friends and family. By choosing to highlight these amazing responses Mary had, the Lord illustrates to us what saying "yes" to Him looks like. He shows us her willingness, her humility, her pursuit for direction, her submission to it, her denial of self, her commitment to bear the cost, and her follow through.

Based on Mary's response to God, I believe many of us have given God our intentions, but not our "yes". What we do after our initial excitement shows if we actually said "yes" to God.

How often have we known someone (or have been that someone) who shared something like "God said I am to _____" and then never completed the task? Or maybe they started and stopped? Maybe you're like me and have done bits of it over the years but never went all-in? When we first get a word from the Lord, we often meet Him with excitement, faith, and emotions. We rejoice, cry, run around the church, and brag about it to others. But we don't often realize the full implications of what is being asked of us. Too often we are not counting the cost (See Luke 14:28.) This results in compromised, incomplete, or never begun journeys that miss the promises and blessings God had in store for our future.

THE GIFT WITHOUT THE COST

Every promise requires sacrifice. Yet, we often want the promise without the sacrifice, and the gifts without the cost.

> "Following (Jesus) may mean we lose relationships, dreams, material things, or even our lives. Those who are following Jesus simply for what they can get won't stick around when the going gets tough. When God's way conflicts with our way, we will feel betrayed by the shallow, me-first faith we have bought into. If we have not counted the cost of being His child, we will turn away at the threat of sacrifice and find something else to gratify our selfish desires". [4]

The costs that come when you commit to the Lord aren't always ones you prepare for, and the honor of taking them on doesn't always feel as glorious as we dream them to be. Christians often dramatically boast saying they will do anything for the Lord no matter what happens. Then, when the thing that matters happens and it's more than what we were willing to do, it simply reveals the secret heart held inside which was more like, "I'll do anything that doesn't cost me much."

We have a "microwave" mindset where we want things instantly. But that's not how the call of God works. We don't get to adopt callings. A child cannot be birthed without going through labor. We don't get to choose the measure of sacrifice we will face, we only choose our response to them. Mary had to carry Jesus for nine long months. She bore every pain, shouldered every criticism, and endured great hardship and loss. That wasn't easy.

We must align ourselves with God's Word, and remind ourselves who He is and the supreme value of what is at stake, His glory being revealed to the nations. So, like a football player facing a blow, get into position, dig your heels into the ground, get your game face on, brace yourself, and determine by God's grace that you will not fall!

RUNNING, STALLING OR WEARY?

We are either running away or toward something/someone. To whom or what are you running? Some of us have received prophecy in the past and said "no" to God. Perhaps like Jonah, you have heard the voice of the Lord and have taken off in the other direction. Jonah didn't just give God a verbal no, his heart and body posture was turned away from God, headed the opposite way. We run either because the call scares us, costs us, or we just don't want it. So, we choose to resist God. If your comfort is an idol (comes before the Lord) then dethrone it. Get before the true King with fear and trembling in total surrender. The eternal glory of satisfying the Holy Spirit far outweighs the temporal joy of gratifying the flesh.

Perhaps you didn't literally refuse, but your actions did. When we stall, drag our feet, and hold up the process, like procrastination, it is a form of saying no. Some of us procrastinate because we struggle with insecurity, doubt, low self-esteem, and even word curses. These issues sometime cause us to withhold ourselves from the fullness of God's plans and we never really say yes. If this is you, seek God who heals and restores true identity. He wants to heal you.

Some of us procrastinate because we are lazy and lack discipline. This is changed only by choosing to put our flesh into submission and to become selfless. If you have opposed God in any form, you need to repent and turn from any oppositional position to a surrendered one.

The incubation period of our calling is determined by the Lord. It can be months, years, or even decades. When preparing this word, the Lord said to me, "For some of you, pregnancy has made you weary. You're worn out from the cost my call has taken." The load has weakened your soul and your will. You have slowed down, and some have even stopped. You have slowly rotated into a positional "no". Whatever the reason, beloved, seek the Lord who heals, strengthens, and restores. He will put things in the right order, He will heal your heart and in Him, you can find rest. Turn around and give God your yes again.

NURTURING THE CALL

After we set ourselves in agreement with God, there is something crucial we must do, find our Elizabeth. Part of nurturing the call is to evaluate who and what you surround yourself with.

> "At that time Mary got ready and hurried to a town in the hill country of Judea, where she entered Zechariah's home and greeted Elizabeth. When Elizabeth heard Mary's greeting, the baby leaped in her womb, and Elizabeth was filled with the Holy Spirit. In a loud voice she exclaimed: "Blessed are you among women, and blessed is the child you will bear! But why am I so favored, that the mother of my Lord should come to me? As soon as the sound of your greeting reached my ears, the baby in my womb leaped for joy. Blessed is she who has believed that the Lord would fulfill his promises to her!" – (Luke 1:39-45 NIV)

Mary never had a chance to tell Elizabeth what had happened to her. The Holy Spirit revealed to Elizabeth who Mary was and the promise she carried within. God will send you an Elizabeth, someone who will bear witness to the call on your life, who will hold you accountable to that call and celebrate you! While Elizabeth and Mary have different callings, they are both pregnant with purpose, and Elizabeth is already producing the fruit of the impossible. This is likely extremely encouraging to Mary. She went from being judged and alone, to a place where she is celebrated and connected with a like-minded friend. Who are you surrounded by?

Listen, lions don't roam around with chickens, they roam with other lions. Amos 3:3 (NIV) says, *"Do two walk together unless they have agreed to do so?"* No! Get with your kind. Find someone who will be honest with you, love you, encourage you, even kick you in the butt if you need them to. Elizabeth knew Mary was carrying the greatest promise ever but she wasn't intimidated or jealous. She was excited and honored! Who is honored to be around you?

God will place mature Christians around you to help call out and encourage what is in you but you must be transparent and vulnerable with them. I know firsthand how scary this can feel, yet God designed us to be a body for a reason. Ask God to send you your Elizabeth. Some of you need to be an Elizabeth, because that is your calling.

IT'S TIME TO SAY YES

If we truly were honest before God, some of us would confess "Lord, if I truly believed and agreed with your Word, I would act differently." What God illustrates to us through Mary is a picture of someone who agrees with Him from beginning to end, staying committed and faithful to the call all the way to completion. She didn't give up or change her mind. She didn't compromise herself or the Lord's words. She had follow-through, commitment, perseverance, discipline, and focus. Even when she faces the threat of losing loved ones, a home, security, she says yes. When she faces persecution, accusations, gossip, and slander, she says yes. When the burden is heavy, when there are sleepless nights, when the pain comes and her flesh wants to give up, she says yes. With every crashing wave, she anchors her heart in the Lord's word.

Like Mary, we must set ourselves in agreement with what God says about us and for us through confession, prayer, and preparation. We must allow God to complete the incubation time of the call, while nurturing and maturing it. We must count the costs, and shoulder them as they come. One evening, the Lord spoke this word to me for women, I pray you receive it:

> God says *"I choose you as daughters. I called you to carry out my will. No more hiding. No more doubting. No more fears. It's time. I chose you to carry my Son. What will your response be? Will it be 'but God...' or will it be 'As you have said, let it be done in me'?".*

Give God your YES!

My name is Rachel Ketchens,
and I am a JESUS Girl.

Rachel Ketchens is an ordained minister and an entrepreneur in the graphic design and marketing industry. She was called to the ministry in 2011 and began preaching at the young age of 23. Rachel is one of the founding church planters of Christ For All Nations Church, where she currently serves as the Children's and Youth Pastor. She also serves as one of the leaders of Sunday Morning Gravy International prayer call. Rachel travels and ministers nationally with How to Heal the Sick conferences and JESUS Girl conferences and lives to serve God and others with the love of Jesus Christ.

CHAPTER 7

Joanna

INSPIRED GIVING & KINGDOM BUILDING

Luke is the only book in the Bible where we see Joanna's name mentioned. Luke tells us she was present at the tomb of Jesus. Other books of the gospels do not mention her or the fact that women supported Jesus' ministry. However, all the gospels give an account of women being present when Jesus was crucified.

Although there was very little written about Joanna, much can be said about her. In Luke 8, we learn that Joanna as well as other women gave from their personal finances to support Jesus' ministry. Her devotion to Jesus stems from being healed from the infirmity in her body. Because of her healing, she felt compelled to give to and support the work Jesus was doing.

Here are a few ways Joanna modeled how we should be as givers and followers of Jesus:

JOANNA GAVE WITHOUT SEEKING ACKNOWLEDGEMENT OR RECOGNITION.

Even when other women were being noticed more than her, she wasn't envious and never stopped giving. Joanna means, "The Lord is grace" or "The Lord gives graciously."[1] She lived up to the meaning of her name. In addition, she yielded to Jesus' teaching. Joanna examined her motives and kept them in check. Matthew 6:1 (TPT) says, *"Examine your motives to make sure you're not showing off when you do your good deeds, only to be admired by others; otherwise, you will lose the reward of your heavenly Father."*

Joanna willingly and joyfully gave because she recognized the importance of spreading the good news about the kingdom of God. Being acknowledged for her giving wasn't important to her. When we give, we should have the same mindset of expanding the kingdom. Even in today's church culture, some will not contribute if they feel they aren't being recognized for their actions. Without understanding the true principle of scriptural giving, they feel they are giving a contribution to the church, not to God's kingdom. Joanna was able to witness Jesus preaching and proclaiming the good news throughout cities and villages. (See Luke 8.) Because of her and the other women's giving, Jesus and the disciples were able to spread the good news to the cities of that area.

Joanna trusted God with her giving.

Some people limit their giving due to a lack of trust in the pastor or leadership. In Jesus' ministry, Judas, the financial overseer, not only betrayed Jesus but also stole money that was put into the ministry.

Joanna didn't stop giving just because Judas was corrupt. She faithfully continued to give trusting that Jesus knew what Judas was doing.

"Then Jesus shocked them with these words: 'I have hand-picked you to be my twelve, knowing that one of you is the devil.' Jesus was referring to Judas Iscariot, son of Simon for he knew that Judas, one of his chosen disciples was getting ready to betray him." (John 6:70-71 TPT)

This shows how much Joanna trusted Jesus and believed in His teaching. Especially in Proverbs 11:28 (TPT), *"Keep trusting in your riches and down you'll go! But the lovers of God rise up like flowers in the spring."* Her love for Jesus was greater than her love for money. She believed the scripture that says, *"No one can serve two masters."* (Matthew 6:24a NIV) Either she would serve God or money, but she knew that she could not serve both.

Joanna reminds us to trust God and listen to Him before regarding other things in our lives including giving, even if things don't look right from our perspective. Proverbs 3:5 (TPT) says, *"Trust in the Lord completely, and do not rely on your own opinions. With all your heart rely on him to guide you, and he will lead you in every decision you make."* With her trust in Jesus, Judas' mismanaging money didn't keep her from giving.

Jesus' twelve disciples had to give up everything, including their incomes, to follow Jesus and be His disciples. Luke 5:11 tells us that Peter left everything behind to follow Jesus. Matthew left in the middle of working to follow Jesus. Giving, by women like Joanna, was critically important to the work of the ministry because it helped provide for the practical needs Jesus and the twelve disciples had for themselves and the ministry ahead.

The work of a pastor goes far beyond five days, forty hours a week. Having an additional corporate job is next to impossible. Their most important focus is advancing the kingdom and caring for their congregation. Their income comes from a portion of the giving of the congregation to the church. We are all part of the ministry when we give.

Joanna gave despite cultural norms, her position in society, and the risks to her and her family.

We know, based on the way Jesus treated and interacted with women, that He held them in high regard and cared for them equally. Jesus valued women in his life from birth, during his time in ministry and when He was resurrected. But this was certainly not the cultural norm. During the first century, women were overlooked. They were treated as second-class citizens whose primary roles were homemaker and child producer. When women went out in public, they were required to abide by certain standards such as only being seen and not heard. Women could not divorce their husbands or hold any legal status in the courts. One of the biggest rules was that women were very limited as to what they could learn or study about God. All of these reasons made Joanna someone that wouldn't likely have been around Jesus. A woman giving anything to Him would have been frowned upon.

It wasn't likely for Joanna to give just because she was a woman, but also who she was connected to. Joanna was married to Chuza, the manager of Herod's household. In fact, she and her husband were servants to Herod Antipas. Herod ruled Galilee during the time of Jesus' ministry. In Luke 13:32, we see that Herod is determined to kill Jesus. By giving to and following Jesus, Joanna not only put herself at risk, but also her family.

When she would speak about Jesus and what she was learning, she had to do it in secret. If the rulers found out what Joanna was doing, Chuza could have lost his position with Herod or even been killed. Nonetheless, even though she was a servant under Herod Antipas' command, she didn't conform to his beliefs or his ways.

Could this be said for Christians today? Whether at a job, school, or even dinner with friends, we can find ourselves in circumstances where people disregard Jesus' teachings.

Are we willing to risk it all for Jesus? When I was a babe in Christ, I wouldn't stand up for my beliefs in fear of not being accepted. Now, I find myself sharing my faith even with people that question Jesus' identity and teachings. As Christians, it is important that we take a stand for what we believe. Like Joanna, we have to remain faithful and have the mindset that is ready to risk it all to follow Jesus.

Throughout Jesus' ministry, Joanna not only gave financially, she also served Him. I couldn't imagine following Jesus and not serving Him. In Luke 24, we see that Joanna and the other women watched Jesus being crucified. It was traditional for women to clean and prepare the body for burial. That Sunday morning, they went to the tomb to prepare His body with fragrant spices and ointments. This act of service requires much strength and compassion, especially when you think of the condition of Jesus' body. It also showed how much they honored and loved Him.

Later on, in Luke 24, Joanna and the other women were the first to witness the empty tomb and share the good news of Jesus' resurrection. Joanna and the other women ran back to tell the remaining disciples about what they had seen and heard. What an honor that Jesus would reveal Himself to the women first.

Joanna gave out of love and obedience to the Word.

Joanna gave out of love and obedience to the Word of God. She didn't give expecting anything in return. She gave from a pure heart which brought glory to our Father. We should do the same with our giving as we let it flow from a pure heart. Giving freely to God and His kingdom should be our joy and pleasure. *"So let each one give as he purposes in his heart, not grudgingly or of necessity; for God loves a cheerful giver."* (2 Corinthians 9:7 NKJV) Through it all, we should give our all because God gave His Son, and Jesus gave His life for us. *"For God so loved the world, that he gave his one and only Son,"* (John 3:16a NIV)

In giving, we honor God and express our gratitude because we truly owe Him everything. In giving to the kingdom, we can witness lives, communities and even nations being changed. Giving is more than supplying for a financial need. Giving can also include our time to expand the kingdom of God. Time like money is a gift from God and it's important that we give Him back what He has given us. Giving time for the kingdom is necessary for growth and witnessing as well as serving others.

GIVING IS KINGDOM-BUILDING

Growing up, I didn't understand the importance of giving. I just knew that the offering was a part of church culture. I would always give a couple dollars, but I never gave God my best despite all He had done for me. In addition, I neglected to give my time to God because I was caught up with worldly things. I was often consumed with work, distracted by social media or involved in social gatherings. I failed at giving God my time. I did what I wanted without spending time with Him or for His work.

I wasn't taught how to be a good steward over the finances and time God had given me. It wasn't until 2016, that I understood the importance of expanding the kingdom through stewardship and having plenty to give.

Giving God our first and best is important. Our tithe is giving back or returning what God has already given to us. *"A tithe of everything from the land, whether grain from the soil or fruit from the trees, belongs to the Lord; it is holy to the Lord"* (Leviticus 27:30 NIV). Also, Proverbs 3:9

(TPT) states, *"Glorify God with all your wealth, honoring him with your very best, with every increase that comes to you."* In addition to giving tithes, giving an offering is also important to God.

Because they lack understanding or obedience in giving to the kingdom of God, many Christians give very little or not at all. Remember, Joanna was constantly gaining understanding and knowledge because she placed herself in position to hear the teaching of Jesus. Pastors, never assume everyone understands why giving to the kingdom is important. I didn't understand until I was in my thirties and wasn't a faithful tither until 2016.

Some people don't give because they feel as if their small amount would not make a difference. Luke 21:1-4 talks about how Jesus observed people while they were giving. There was a widow that gave only two copper coins while the rich gave their larger gifts. Yet, Jesus stressed that the poor widow gave more than others because she gave her all. She gave everything.

Don't worry about who is looking at you and don't worry about how much you give Him, just trust and obey God with your giving and watch Him bless you.

My name is Jennifer Lee,
and I am a JESUS Girl.

Jennifer Lee grew up being active in the church where she discovered her love for dance. She has led and participated with several dance ministries as well as taught dance workshops throughout Missouri and Illinois. While attending Lincoln University in Jefferson City, Missouri she received professional dance training. In 2016, God led her to Christ For All Nations, where she accepted the call to preach the Word of God. Jennifer also serves in deliverance ministry where she is able to partner in prayer with people for their spiritual freedom. In the summer of 2018, Jennifer received her master's degree in education from Central Methodist University.

CHAPTER 8

The Unclean Woman
DESPERATION

*"In the crowd that day was a woman who had suffered greatly
for twelve years from slow bleeding. Even though she had spent
all that she had on healers, she was still suffering. Pressing in
through the crowd, she came up behind Jesus and touched the
tassel of his prayer shawl. Instantly her bleeding stopped and
she was healed.*

*Jesus suddenly stopped and said to his disciples, 'Someone
touched me. Who is it?'*

*While they all denied it, Peter pointed out, 'Master, everyone is
touching you, trying to get close to you. The crowds are so thick
we can't walk through all these people without being jostled.'*

Jesus replied, 'Yes, but I felt power surge through me. Someone touched me to be healed, and they received their healing.'

When the woman realized she couldn't hide any longer, she came and fell trembling at Jesus' feet. Before the entire crowd she declared, 'I was desperate to touch you, Jesus, for I knew if I could just touch even the fringe of your robe I would be healed.'

Jesus responded, 'Beloved daughter, your faith in me has released your healing. You may go with my peace.'"[1]

LABELED

There is so much revelation and depth in this story that it is impossible to uncover it all. This may even be considered one of the most well-known stories in the Bible. I have heard this story preached so many times and yet, this time, I realized we do not know anything about this woman's life. We do not know her name, if she had a husband, family or friends, or what she did for a living. All we know is that she was labeled by this infirmity. Most of her story seems to be left to the imagination. However, one thing is true in the end: she walked away whole and with more of Jesus Christ.

I wonder how she felt during the twelve years she dealt with this issue, especially when put into an historical context. Back then, women who were in the process of menstruation, as well as women who had unrelated issues of blood flow, were considered unclean. Not only that, everything and everyone they came into contact with was considered unclean as well, even their husbands.

"If a woman has a flow of blood for many days that is unrelated to her menstrual period, or if the blood continues beyond the normal period, she is ceremonially unclean. As during her menstrual period, the woman will be unclean as long as the

discharge continues. Any bed she lies on and any object she sits on during that time will be unclean, just as during her normal menstrual period. If any of you touch these things, you will be ceremonially unclean. You must wash your clothes and bathe yourself in water, and you will remain unclean until evening."[2]

Imagine being labeled "unclean" for twelve long years. I imagine people gave up on her over the course of time. Perhaps, they were okay with going through the motions of ceremonially cleaning themselves for the first few months, but soon grew tired of the process. I think of how lonely she would have become if people who had once been there for her stopped visiting. She probably had no one to confide in, which left her feeling rejected. Those she relied on in the past may have abandoned her because being with her was too much of a hassle.

REJECTED

I am sure we can all go back to a time in our lives in which we felt rejected like her. We can think of people who either said they would always be there for us, or people who were supposed to be there for us. It could be siblings, a mother, a father, a trusted friend, or even a husband. We could easily identify with this woman. No one is immune to rejection.

Personally, rejection is something I battled with all my life. I am dark-skinned. While I was growing up, other kids often made fun of me. They constantly asked me why I was so "black," and told me that I was ugly because I was so dark. I remember coming home and telling my parents what happened and, of course, they told me there was nothing wrong with my skin tone. They told me to tell the other kids, "The blacker the berry, the sweeter the juice." That did not go over well with the other kids because then, I was both dumb and ugly.

As I got older, when I was not being taunted about my skin color, it was because of my size. I was never skinny and have always been a thick girl. I was encouraged to go on diet after diet during the summer breaks from school, but was unable to stick to any of them. In fact, I ended up hating myself more because I felt as if I would never look right (whatever "right" was). I struggled with all of this on top of the pressure I felt as a pastor's daughter.

While battling these internal struggles about how I looked and who I was, everyone felt it necessary to judge and comment on my choices. When I made choices that were different from those they would have made, I was looked down upon and judged harshly. Honestly, I felt defeated and as if nothing I ever did was good enough. This always made me feel worse because I was always striving for perfection. However, I thought I had some kind of advantage because at least I could hide *most* of my problems.

DEFEATED

So, I began to think about this woman and how defeated she felt because she could not hide her problems at all. When people saw her, they knew exactly what her problem was. I thought of her shame and embarrassment. On top of this, all the money she saved up was used on "healers" - people she thought could save her from her suffering and misery. Sadly, nothing ever worked. She still went back home in agony. She had all of her heart issues - rejection, abandonment, embarrassment, disappointment, possibly even self-hatred, compounded with this physically taxing sickness.

DESPERATE

I am sure she felt low and hopeless. Then one day, she began hearing rumors of a man named Jesus who worked miracles. I often wonder if she believed in the Messiah and thought, "Finally, my Hope has come!" Maybe she was not a believer at first, but others' testimonies and stories touched something deep within her. Whichever it was, it ignited a desperation inside of her. A desperation not just to be made whole, but she says herself in the passage in Luke - a desperation to touch Jesus. We see that in her desperation to touch Jesus, He responded, and then she was made whole. Jesus' response yielded wholeness inside as well as out.

I firmly believe that God responded to her *because* she was desperate for Him. This excerpt of this woman's life clues us in on something important to God. He does not just want us to need Him because we know we need Him, we should want Him. The passage goes even further. The woman with the issue of blood did not say she wanted to touch Jesus, she said she was desperate to touch Him!

There is a difference between wanting something and being desperate for something. As people, we acknowledge that we want something all the time, but we do not necessarily do anything about it. However, if someone says they are desperate for something, they put action behind it. I believe God wants His people (including His girls) to be truly desperate for Him, but it requires a certain move on our part. It is not just about our emotions, but also about our actions. Desperation is an action word! This woman was so desperate that she pressed in through a massive crowd just to touch Jesus' tassel and walked away whole.

I thought about the word "desperate" and decided to look it up in the dictionary. One of the definitions is "having a great need or desire for something."[3] However, I thought if we are talking about being desperate for God, it would have to mean more than this, or at least the definition would be a little different. So, I asked the Lord to show me what desperation looks like and how He would define it. He sent me to Psalm 63:1-8 in the Passion Translation. It says,

"For the Pure and Shining One

King David's song when he was exiled in the Judean wilderness.
O God of my life, I'm lovesick for you in this weary wilderness.
I thirst with the deepest longings to love you more,
with cravings in my heart that can't be described.
Such yearning grips my soul for you, my God!
I'm energized every time I enter
your heavenly sanctuary to seek more of your power
and drink in more of your glory.
For your tender mercies mean more to me than life itself.
How I love and praise you, God!
Daily I will worship you passionately and with all my heart.
My arms will wave to you like banners of praise.
I overflow with praise when I come before you,
for the anointing of your presence satisfies me like nothing else.
You are such a rich banquet of pleasure to my soul.
I lie awake each night thinking of you
and reflecting on how you help me like a father.
I sing through the night under your splendor-shadow,
offering up to you my songs of delight and joy!
With passion I pursue and cling to you.
Because I feel your grip on my life,
I keep my soul close to your heart."[4]

I love King David's heartfelt declaration of love and pursuit in this passage to the Lord. He is crying out to the Lord in his desperation. The words he says are actions he takes because he is hungry for God. He thirsts to love God more. He talks about how he loves and praises God, and how he will worship Him daily. He speaks of waving his arms like banners of praise, lying awake each night thinking of the Lord, singing through the night to Him and about Him, and how he pursues Him with passion. This is what desperation for God looks like.

INTIMACY

There are so many steps we can take to increase our hunger and desperation for the Lord in our walk. All the actions David mentioned are meant to be practical. Doing these things, and even incorporating others, are ways to increase our intimacy with the Lord. As we seek to increase intimacy with Him - knowing Him and allowing Him to know us - our hunger and desperation for Him will also increase.

One simple way is to adopt a different routine in the morning when you wake. The first thing we normally do is check our phones and go about our days. In the morning, in that first moment after you open your eyes, try telling God, Jesus, and the Holy Spirit "Good morning!" Tell them that you love them. Thank God for waking you up. Give God the honor of being the first person you talk to every day. It is His breath that fills our lungs. The least we could do is make sure that when He chooses - out of His infinite mercy and love - to wake us up with our hearts beating and our lungs fully functional that we give that breath back to Him. Remember *"For in Him we live, and move, and have our being..."*[5]

TRANSPARENCY

In addition to taking these steps to increase intimacy with God, desperation also requires transparency on our part. The woman with the issue of blood had to be transparent in order for Jesus to make her whole. I could imagine how embarrassed she already was and then, she was put on the spot. Still, the scripture says she was desperate to touch Jesus and that she knew if she could touch Him, she would be healed.

In her transparency, she did not care what people thought of her or how they looked at her. I am sure they were looking at her because the Bible says, *"she came and fell trembling at Jesus' feet..."* She had to be making some kind of scene because falling draws attention.

However, she was willing to push past any sort of embarrassment and stares because there was healing in her transparency. Not only did she fall at His feet, but it says that she declared her desperation and what Jesus did for her before the entire crowd. Everyone had literally seen her at her worst and then she had to give her testimony to everyone. Her desperation for Christ outweighed any embarrassment she felt.

Considering the possibility of public humiliation gave me a flashback to my past. I struggled with things like addiction, unforgiveness, trauma, and all kinds of perversion for years. But I went to church every Sunday! It took me eighteen long years to be transparent enough to confess that I had any problem. Being transparent about my issues to someone else who pointed me to Christ brought about the inner healing I desperately longed for. It was a healing I did not even know how to articulate that I needed.

Simply initially admitting my issues wasn't the end of the transparency. In fact, it was only just the beginning. Eventually, I had to tell my testimony in front of others, not just for the sake of being transparent, but so that my transparency might also bring healing, deliverance, and salvation to others. In my desperation to be made whole, I humbled myself (which was a testimony all on its own) and for the first time in my life, I wasn't concerned with how I looked to other people.

Being transparent is definitely a risk. However, I can assure you that taking this risk will bring about wonderful spiritual growth and change in you and the people to whom you share your testimony. Being transparent in this way makes room for God to be God in your life and in the lives of others.

In the passage of scripture, Jesus wanted to know who touched Him. He knew exactly who it was, but He wanted her to publicly acknowledge her healing. Right after this, it also says that she knew she could not hide any longer. There are people who need to hear what God has done for you. They cannot receive what they need if you remain hidden and silent, and neither can you.

Being transparent does not make you weak. Transparency includes being both humble and bold. Desperation looks at the potential for embarrassment and shame in the face and says, "So what if they know everything?" In that desperation, there is also a transparency with God. It allows us to come to Him no matter how embarrassed, guilty, or ashamed we may feel. He wants us to come to Him with everything and lay it all at His feet. Just as the woman did, we should even lay ourselves at His feet and tell Him how we desperately need Him.

OBEDIENCE

Desperation requires transparency about everything, including where we are in our walk with Him, but it also requires fearing the Lord. I do not mean being scared of someone who is out to get you. Fearing the Lord means having awe and reverence for Him, worshipping Him, and submitting to Him. In Proverbs 1:7, The Passion Translation simply calls it an obedient devotion to God. Obedience comes out of fearing Him. It is impossible to say you fear the Lord if you never obey His Word.

Obedience simply starts with obeying what you know. Do not focus on the things you do not know or understand. Simply start with the Ten Commandments. (See Exodus 20:1-17.) Using the commandments, run a check of your heart to see if you have kept His law.

When God gives us a commandment, He does not want us to respond by huffing, sighing, and dragging our feet. We hate it when we tell kids to do something and they respond with this kind of reaction. We find it rude and disrespectful. Truth be told, some of us (I know I do) just tell them "Never mind", simply because we do not like their attitude. Thankfully, God is not like this with us, He patiently waits for us to obey. Still, we (like children) do not understand God is telling us to obey Him in these matters for our own good.

When it comes to obedience, He wants us to react like the writer of the Psalms did when he said, "I delight to do Your will, O my God, and Your law *is* within my heart."[7] He wants us to have joy in our obedience. He wants it to become our pleasure to obey Him. Part of that may be adjusting our attitudes when it comes to His laws and commands. These are not just a list of rules for us to follow. They are part of an agreement to be faithful to Him. Obedience to God ignites a desperation and a longing for His ways.

Kids can only get certain privileges and promises from us when they are being obedient and have a good attitude. The same is true with the Father. There are special blessings and promises for those who are obedient. Obedience builds trust and creates intimacy. Intimacy with God is the entire goal. Not only that, if we love God, we will willingly and faithfully obey Him. The Bible says to obey Him quickly. Remember, any delay in doing the things God has commanded us to do is disobedience. We get irritated when our kids take too long to do what we have told them to, likewise, we should not make Him wait either.

AGREEMENT

Being desperate for Jesus also requires total agreement with His Word. By His Word, I mean the Bible and everything in it. This also includes words He has spoken over us or through someone else. It is difficult to obey something with which you do not agree. The Bible says that the Word is God. Since the Word is God, then God must be His Word. When there is a lack of agreement with His Word, there is a lack of agreement with Him. It is impossible for any two people to walk together through life unless they agree. (See Amos 3:3.)

Disagreeing with His Word may not always look like you do not believe something. It may also look like you are picking and choosing the parts of His Word that suit you, or do not offend you. It is leaving the parts that offend you or do not suit your lifestyle on the table. In doing this, you are rejecting the One who is the Word - Jesus Christ. You are also fashioning idols for yourselves - a god to suit your own needs and desires. If you say you love Him, or if you want to love Him, you must be lovers of His Word. *Some* of Him is not good enough. You must take *all* of Him.

If you have trouble understanding how God views some things, consider this. I always find it helps me if I think about it in the aspect of a parent and their child. No one humbles you more than a child. For example, we expect our children to follow our household rules. They may express a dislike for some of those rules while others may not bother them. One day, they could say they do not mind taking a bath before bedtime because it is convenient. They could also add they do not like the rule of cleaning their bedrooms. As a parent, we would tell them there is no choice. It is all or nothing. Take it or leave it. It is the same way with God - take it all. If you find yourself in disagreement with God's Word, just be transparent and honest with the Lord, and tell Him in prayer. Allow Him to heal and deal with your heart.

SURRENDER

Finally, all of these aforementioned things - intimacy, transparency, fear of the Lord, obedience, and agreement - require humble submission and surrender. This is really where desperation begins. It is all in your willingness to surrender to God. Surrender requires laying aside of all pride. This includes the pride of life, the pride of thinking you know better and would do a better job than God if you were in control. Surrender calls for you to humble yourself and give ALL of you over to God. This also requires a relinquishing of all control, a total trust, confidence in, and reliance upon who God is. It is the image of a baby, who can do nothing on their own and is totally reliant upon their parents. It takes humility to surrender and submit.

The truth is we do not know better and cannot do a better job than God. We do not even know what we do not know, but God knows everything. We should submit to Him out of reverence for who He is. He is an omniscient and holy King who deserves our confidence and trust. When we are truly desperate for someone, we lay down our self-interest and do whatever that person wants simply because it pleases them. Desperation demands denying self and picking up Christ.

Desperation for God is something that can never be totally listed or understood. That said, there are countless fruits that desperation should produce. Desperation for God requires the supernatural grace of God. It is an act of mercy that God would impart to us a desperation for Him. Yet, it still requires action on our part.

What does your desperation look like?

What are you willing to do?

Are you willing to submit and surrender?

What is the crowd that you have to press through?

It could be circumstances, emotions, people's opinions of you, or a schedule. I assure you, God is worth it. Desperation does not look the same for everybody, but it still produces the same kind of fruit: intimacy, transparency, fear of the Lord, obedience, total agreement with God's Word, humble submission and surrender to God. All of this should be done in a relentless pursuit of Him. Our prize in being desperate for the Lord is simply Him and to behold Him as He is and as He wants to be - our everything.

My name is Amber Owens,
and I am a JESUS Girl.

Amber Owens is an educator and minister. She was born, raised, and educated in St. Louis, Missouri. She holds bachelor's degrees in film studies and forensic science. In 2014, she accepted her call to ministry and was ordained two years later. Amber currently works for the Special School District of Missouri. She is a daughter of Christ For All Nations Church in Belleville, Illinois and gives all glory to God for completely transforming her life.

CHAPTER 9

Testimonies of

MODERN-DAY JESUS GIRLS

In October 2012, I got a job as a supervisor for a company. I knew this job would be temporary. As time went on, I realized God must have placed me there for a reason. I did not know what that reason could have been at the time so I asked God. He began giving me clear answers in many different ways throughout 2012 to 2014. God revealed my purpose at this job in more ways than one which was such confirmation. The one that stood out the most became my greatest testimony.

In June of 2014, I started having a rough time with some of my co-workers. They were rebellious, uncooperative, and disrespectful to the employer. It got to the point where I started to seek employment elsewhere. I prayed and asked God for direction. I wanted another job. As I sat quietly at my desk waiting to hear the voice of the Lord, I became frustrated with distractions. I knew at that moment, I needed be alone, so I immediately shut the door.

God spoke to me and said, "You will be working this job for five more years."

I immediately started having a panic attack. The tears of disappointment and disbelief started flowing heavily down my face. I was so upset that I had to go home for the rest of the day. I was crying as if I was a child getting the ultimate punishment. Once I got home and tried to relax, God spoke again.

He said, "I will never leave you. I am always with you."

I immediately got quiet to take it all in. At this stage of my life, everything with my job was so overwhelming that I really wanted to quit. From 2014 to 2016, I started seeing changes and experiencing stages of growth. I got married in 2014 and separated in 2016. While all that was happening, I stood on the promises of God.

By this time, I could tell my co-workers were comfortable with their negative behaviors and going against company policies. Ignoring God's message, I started applying for other positions. Every door or window of opportunity closed, with the explanation that I was either over qualified or didn't have enough experience.

As life continued in 2016, I lost a best friend to colon cancer. I often vented to her on a regular basis about my job and my separation from my husband. In March of 2017, my divorce was final. It seemed all I could do was grieve the loss of my friend, think about my ex-husband and a job I was unhappy with. I went to God in prayer for immediate help. I sincerely asked Him for healing and strength. By mid 2017, I repeated multiple prayers asking not only for healing and strength, but for opportunities to help someone else. I truly wanted God to get all the glory, honor and praise.

Just when things started to calm down in my life, my daughter was diagnosed with Lupus, my step-mother with cancer, and my grandmother with Parkinson's disease. The news of all three diagnoses within such a short time was mentally draining. After doctor visits, hospital visits, many prayers, fasting and talking to God, my job (that I was very disappointed with) became my pillar of strength.

People would say, "You show yourself strong, how do you do it?"

My response would be the same every time, "It is nothing but the grace of God."

In 2019, my daughter, step-mother and grandmother passed away within two weeks of each other. The company I worked for was there for me, ready and willing to give me full support and time off as I needed it. I thanked God for blessing me with that work flexibility to move around and get things done.

Later in 2019, I received a phone call from someone asking me to send over my resume. I was hesitant because I remembered exactly what God spoke and this time I wanted to walk in obedience. I plugged in my flash drive and noticed the date when I last updated the information. The revision took place five years prior.

I said, "Okay! God is this YOU?!"

God gave me the okay to move forward with the process of my new job. Because of my experience, I was offered two positions on a supervisory level. I prayed about it before I gave the company an answer. I was finally allowing God to direct me. I chose to make a faith-move and start from the bottom at the new company. In my new position, I am around people I am able to help and to God be the glory.

We never know how things will happen but we do know God has a strategic way of working them out. I give God all the praise for allowing little old me to be a help to someone else. Even though I've been through a lot, I am able to clearly see that God has given me the peace, comfort, healing and strength I prayed for. Always remember to, *"Trust in the Lord with all thine heart; and lean not unto thine own understanding. In all thy ways acknowledge him, and he shall direct thy path"* (Proverbs 3:5-6 KJV). Always remember, God's got you!

My name is LaToya,
and I am a JESUS Girl.

I was living in south Florida with my lesbian girlfriend who started being verbally and physically abusive towards me. Not only was the abuse wearing on me, so was the homosexual lifestyle. A dear friend of mine had repeatedly invited me to a 30-day consecration church service being held at the church she attended. I would always decline and make an excuse as to why I couldn't go.

Monday, June 22, 1998, was a day I will never forget. My dear friend didn't have to call me because I showed up at her house. As she opened the door, I wailed out of weariness. She prayed with me and encouraged me to come to church. This time I decided I would go.

We went to church and during the invitation to discipleship, I heard the voice of the Lord. I was instantly delivered from homosexuality. As the church counselor began to pray with me, I felt very nauseous. I told the counselor how I was feeling and she told me to go to the bathroom. Instead, I went outside. As soon as I got there, I began to vomit uncontrollably. I came back in and told the counselor what happened. She explained to me that I had been delivered. The Lord was purifying and cleansing me, and my life was never the same after that. The Lord set me free!

My name is Trikenya,
and I am a JESUS Girl.

(For more on this subject, see Genesis 2:22-25 which talks about how God made man for woman.)

Ain't God good! This really isn't a question, it is a glorious declaration. It is my response to all the situations I have faced on this journey called life, but it wasn't always. I've learned to trust in Jesus, I've learned to trust in God (in my Andrae Crouch singing voice).[1]

After living on this earth for over 65 years, I have never had an illness or injury so rare or devastating that the wisdom of medical experts could not handle it - Ain't God good!

I have never had to visit my two children in jail - Ain't God good!

After 45 years of marriage, I have never had to deal with issues of infidelity - Ain't God good!

I have never been homeless - Ain't God good!

My testimony is about the awesome deliverance power of God. He is constantly delivering me from myself. God doesn't have to do anything to us...we do it to ourselves. Self-righteousness, self-absorption, self-hate, self-abuse, self-pride, and self-doubt had "sneaked" into my perfect world and threatened to destroy my witness and relationship with Jesus. Satan comes to kill, steal and destroy. Yes, and he will use you if you aren't careful.

Man looks at the outward appearance, but God looks at the heart. Regular church attendance, singing in the choir, going to revivals, attending religious conferences, being a Sunday School teacher and even being married to a pastor was not enough to eradicate the power of selfishness. Those activities are powerless without the sincere desire to please God. The Apostle Paul said it best, *I die daily.*[2] I learned those outward activities occurred only occasionally and that "I" was with "me" every day.

The feelings of loneliness (in a room full of people), the feelings of emptiness (following the praise of people), the feeling of incompleteness (after the event/project was over) kept me seeking answers. Jesus answered by opening my eyes to see what the world couldn't see….my heart! I began to seek Him daily wholeheartedly and He revealed that my self-worth could only be measured by His standards.

My deliverance from myself begins and ends with an attitude of gratitude. Thankfulness is an act of humility towards God. Gratefulness has proven to be a solid foundation to prioritize the very essence of life. Today, my life is hidden in the life of Christ and for that I am eternally grateful.

It is no longer I (self) who lives, but Christ who lives in me.[3] Ain't God good!

My name is Mz. Vickie,
and I am a JESUS Girl.

I watched as the blood slowly ran down my arm. It seemed to creep from my wrist, toward my elbow, and into the small pool collecting on my blanket. I cried so hard and for so long, that I had no more strength to do anything except silently stare at what I had done. My breathing slowed below its normal resting rate, and I finally passed out on my couch.

Sometime later, I woke up to the same scene. I was still alive, and disappointed. I wasn't trying to kill myself this time, or at least I didn't think I was. I only intended to cut myself like I always did. However, this time I had gone a lot deeper with the blade. Perhaps I was trying to leave this world, again. It didn't really matter to me. I had nothing to live for, or so it seemed.

From age 14 to nearly 22, I struggled with depression, severe anxiety, self-mutilation, and suicide attempts. Actually, struggle doesn't seem like the right word. It was more like I was held captive and tortured on a daily basis for their amusement. I tried to self-medicate with drugs, sex, alcohol, partying, overeating, and cutting. Cutting was my daytime medication. It was how I drowned out the thoughts, took back a moment of control over my body, and projected my inward pain to the outside.

I started on my arms and graduated to my thighs because I began to run out of room. I tried real medicine, but it just seemed to make me feel numb and emotionless. For a person with depression, real death seemed better than numbness. I made a few suicide attempts that obviously failed. Twice I was admitted to the psych ward. The frequent anxiety attacks I experienced would cause me to pull off the road and call for help because I couldn't breathe. It seemed like my life was panning out the way I wanted, so I didn't understand why I would spiral into depression.

None of my thoughts were rational or logical. They were often extreme and confusing. I was always sad in my heart. I rarely felt any form of happiness. I was smiling at everyone, yet silently dying inside. I was screaming for help in many subtle and quiet ways hoping someone would hear me, but no one did, except one...Jesus.

At age 21, a seemingly normal looking 20-year-old girl preached the gospel of Jesus Christ to me. She told me God loved me, but the way I was living would send me to hell. Being an atheist (and sometimes agnostic), I got so angry with her that I cried in a rage. She was wrong. There was no God, and if He existed then He didn't care a thing about me or what I did. I was determined to prove her wrong.

So I went to the only church I knew. I went three times and didn't hear or feel anything. Then there was the fourth time. Everything changed. I encountered God Himself! I walked into the church depressed, suicidal, gay, and drug-addicted, and walked out free! Just like that, all at once, Jesus Christ delivered me and saved me. From that moment, I have never looked back or had a desire to return to the world. And from that moment, I never experienced depression, anxiety, cutting, or suicidal thoughts.

I have joy. I smile and laugh all the time because I'm truly happy. God is good. He can free you from anything. I come from deep-rooted generational depression and mental illness in my family. The doctors said this was just a hormonal imbalance, a genetically predetermined disease, but the devil is a liar! I am free today. Nothing is too hard for our God!

My name is Rachel,
and I am a JESUS Girl.

When I was three years old, I went to church every night with my mother, brother and sisters. I began to feel the spirit of the Lord around age five. One day, I was sitting in the church and everyone around me was dancing and shouting.

I said, "Lord, I want to feel what they are feeling."

I prayed so hard and BOOM, just like that, I received the anointed Holy Spirit. It felt like electricity ran from the top of my head to the bottom of my feet. Believe me when I tell you, once you come in contact with Jesus, you will never be the same. I now have the anointing to heal and I believe in and have visions. I have faith that moves mountains, troubles and obstacles.

At fifteen, I remember meeting a very handsome young man and I fell so hard for him. You probably know what comes next. I finally built up enough nerve to ask my mother for birth control pills and she was totally against it. I even tried to have my cousin pose as my mother. That didn't work either. I ended up giving in to the temptation and had sex with him. After just one time, I was pregnant. Of course, he said it wasn't his baby. I was devasted and didn't know what to do. I prayed to God and I spoke to my pastor because I needed answers.

Later, I found out the guy was married and had a baby on the way with his wife. I was in a dark place and the devil knew it. I was so devasted that I want to kill myself and the unborn baby. Over the years, that man had nothing to do with our son and continued to deny paternity.

Even though it was a very dark time, God was faithful. He will always bring us out of the darkness. No matter what obstacles and roadblocks we go through in life, God will bring us out. The devil thought he had gotten hold of me, but God said "No, she is my child." Amen.

The Lord hears your prayers even when you do not think He is listening. I remember I was on my way to an interview one day and a car pulled out in my path. I couldn't stop and slammed into that car. My chest hit the steering wheel and I was rushed to the hospital. I was having excruciating chest pain so they ran all kinds of tests related to the chest and heart.

I remember the doctor coming into my room to ask if I had anybody there with me.

I said, "Yes," but visibly, there was no one.

He said, "We have called in the heart surgeon. You will need emergency heart surgery. Your main artery that flows to your heart is ripped and is leaking." When the doctor left the room, I laid my hand on my chest and began to pray. I called on the name of Jesus and instantly my chest rose up. I was healed by the blood of Jesus.

The doctors came back in the room and said we are going to do another test. When they did, they could not believe their eyes.

They said, "Where did the rip go?"

God sealed it closed. God is real. He is my Savior. I am a living witness and that is my testimony. Amen.

> My name is Dr. Sarah,
> and I am a JESUS Girl.

I visited St. Louis several times to attend a yearly women's conference. During every visit, I felt a tug at my heart. It was a call to move there and serve in inner city ministry. In 2013, I took a huge leap and moved to St. Louis with a prospective job and a mere $700 in cash. Prior to the move, I had undergone a season of financial loss when the economy went south and my employer laid me off. It was a season of learning to trust God as my provider. I immediately began to serve as much as possible at an inner-city church and mission base. Little by little, the Lord increased me and I began to get established. The Lord was providing for me supernaturally and teaching me to trust Him in a way I had never had to before.

In the middle of 2014, my car began to fail. My budget did not allow for all the necessary repairs and I asked the Lord for wisdom. I knew that my budget was too small for a car payment and I didn't have much in savings to purchase even a cheap used car. Then these two scriptures began to rise in my spirit:

"But seek first his kingdom and his righteousness, and all these things will be given to you as well." (Matthew 6:33 NIV)

"And everyone who has left houses or brothers or sisters or father or mother or wife or children or fields for my sake will receive a hundred times as much and will inherit eternal life." (Matthew 19:29 NIV)

I began spending time in God's presence daily. Like a small child, I would sit with Him and love on Him. He continued to show me scriptures from His Word such as: *"If you, then, though you are evil, know how to give good gifts to your children, how much more will your Father in heaven give good gifts to those who ask him!"* (Matthew 7:11 NIV).

My faith began to rise and I was convinced that Papa God was not only able to give me a car but He wanted to give me my heart's desire. He is a good Father and gives good gifts to His children. By faith, I shopped online for my car. I narrowed it down to a White Kia Soul with a panoramic sunroof. It was the first time I had been so precise in my prayers and asked in faith for exactly what I needed and desired. I even began to tell others that God was going to give me a new car.

On September 17, 2015, I was attending a women's conference. To my surprise, the Lord blessed me with my dream car. It was exactly what I had asked for… a 2015 White Kia Soul with a panoramic sunroof. Several leaders from the inner-city ministry church had written a letter regarding my faithfulness to serve and freely give of my time. The conference committee selected me as the recipient of the reward. God orchestrated it every step of the way. He truly is faithful to fulfill His promises and to meet our needs. We simply need to trust Him.

My name is Elaine,
and I am a JESUS Girl.

When we understand who we are in Christ and whose we are, the issues of life become a comfort to our heart. We can begin to see how they happened and how God purposes things for our good. I was ordained and licensed on April 10, 2004. You might say, "Wow, she's been doing ministry for quite some time." Sure, I have years of man's ordination under my belt, but what is more important is the lifetime of God preparing, sanctifying, and teaching me. He waited patiently for this hard-headed young lady who made numerous bad decisions to stop beating herself up.

I wondered, "How could any of this be corrected through a God I only heard about?" My life had not yet displayed Him front and center.

Through many trials and tribulations, I have received an abundance of God's mercy and grace. I now understand these profound verses had been embedded in my heart, mind, and spirit:

"For God so loved the world, that he gave his only begotten Son, that whosoever believeth in him should not perish, but have everlasting life." (John 3:16 KJV)

"But my God shall supply all your need according to his riches in glory by Christ Jesus." (Philippians 4:19 KJV)

"Though he slay me, yet will I hope in him; I will surely defend my ways to his face." (Job 13:15 NIV)

I was a flight attendant for 25 years. During the first five years, God was pursuing me to come back to Him through much chastisement and an overflow of His protection and love. Today, I clearly remember a pair of flannel pajamas I brought on most of my trips during those years. During that season of surrendering my life to God while still entangled with the world, I could not quit smoking. In my hotel room at the Flagship Hotel in Atlantic City, I wanted a cigarette yet knew the Holy Spirit couldn't dwell in an unclean temple. (See 1 Corinthians 6:19.)

God made my salvation clear to me that day; either I receive it or my destiny would be a day of reckoning for me. I was raised to understand when God shows fire in front of you, He is giving you a warning. I usually didn't light my cigarette with a match, but I had no lighter and the temptation of the cigarette was strong. So I grabbed the matches off the hotel table, and without thinking, a spark went straight to my flannel pajamas pants.

My whole right leg went up in flames. I was in shock and assumed my life was over because I was literally on fire. I was prepared for the pain and screaming I thought was about to come from my mouth, knowing no one was there to save me. I fell to the floor begging God to help me. Suddenly, I realized the flames were no more. Shaking out of control, I finally looked at my leg realizing not only was the flame gone but my pajamas were not burned. These were flannel pajamas!

I stayed on the floor and cried out to God saying, "Lord, help me return to You."

This was truly God's mercy and grace coupled with an overflow of His love. I still carry those old flannel pajamas with me to this day as a reminder. The Word of the Lord says, *"And they overcame him by the blood of the Lamb, and by the word of their testimony; and they loved not their lives unto the death."* (Revelations 12:11 KJV)

At that moment, I surrendered all!

My name is Evangelist Wanda,
and I am a JESUS Girl.

I have watched God perform miracle after miracle. I suffered with heavy menstrual cycles, anemia, and fibroids most of my life. In 2005, I got married and my doctor told me if I wanted to have children, I needed to start trying right away. My chance of a successful pregnancy was highly unlikely. Two months later, I was pregnant.

With this pregnancy, I had a fibroid growing along with my baby. I looked like I was carrying twins. The fibroid grew so big, I feared it would suffocate my baby. Because the baby was breach and a fibroid blocked the birth canal, I had to have a C-section. God showed me that He caused her to be breach to save her life and mine. I now have two beautiful children and a bonus child.

In the last couple of years, my menstrual cycles got so bad that I had to be hospitalized and receive blood transfusions. I had surgery to stop my cycles, but it was unsuccessful. So this year, I had to have a hysterectomy. I got very sick after my surgery. I had believed God for healing, and I was so disappointed that I had to have a hysterectomy. God showed me that I was holding on to a lot of unforgiveness, hurt, pain, let downs and disappointments. All that was manifesting through those heavy cycles and fibroids. God wanted me free and free indeed, so He saw fit for the surgery to remove it all.

During my time of resting, God revealed to me so many people and things I had to let go of. He said He was blessing me with a spiritual womb so that I may carry and deliver what He put inside me without any complications. God is still a healer and a miracle worker and I am so grateful for His love and faithfulness!

My name is Latonya,
and I am a JESUS Girl.

I have been going to church my whole life. I was told my grandmother would bring me to her church in a baby carrier. When I was twelve, a pivotal point in my life happened. I loved music and saw the choir getting ready for the Sunday morning worship service. I decided to stay so I could hear the choir sing. During that service, I realized being a church member was not the same as being saved. I joined the church. Later that same day, while I was home, I received salvation by confessing my sins and asking the Lord into my heart and life.

Some months after that experience, I accepted my call into ministry. It was a struggle because the pastor did not believe in or support female preachers. Despite this, I was excited about and tried to live to please God. I did not get caught up in the street life, drugs, sex, addictions or other things. I witnessed family members stuck in these various lifestyles and didn't like how it affected them, our family or me. My struggles were with the hidden issues of depression and suicidal thoughts.

I was saved, but depressed. I tried to pray it away but didn't see a change. I even attempted suicide a few times. I confessed to my best friend what I had done, and she was upset. She began to speak words of encouragement over me.

She said, "Charisse, don't you see the Lord wants you here? He wants to use you. That is why your attempts at suicide were not successful."

After that, I began to find ways to deal with and get healing from my struggle with depression. Even though my battle was not visible, I still struggled. I thank God I did not turn to alcohol, drugs or other addictions to escape my depression. Joyce Meyer's book *Battlefield of the Mind* truly helped me name my struggle. It also taught me how to use the Word of God as a source of help, strength and encouragement when I would get in a low, dark place mentally.

I have read too many stories about Christians and/or clergy committing suicide. As a result, I have been an advocate for encouraging people to go to counseling. Seek help from medical and spiritual professionals. Continue to pray and ask the Lord for help and strength. As I look back over my life, I often reflect on the things I have accomplished.

I think about the many times I have heard someone say to me, "Thank you for sharing your experience. Thank you for allowing the Lord to use you. Thank you for helping me."

It makes me wonder, "What if Satan had won and I succeeded in committing suicide, how different would this world be?"

Then I think I may not be "great" or famous, but I am needed. In the words of the gospel singer Marvin Sapp, "I'm so glad I made it."[4]

My name is Charise,
and I am a JESUS Girl.

"Elisha replied, 'Listen to this message from the Lord! This is what the Lord says: By this time tomorrow in the markets of Samaria, six quarts of choice flour will cost only one piece of silver, and twelve quarts of barley grain will cost only one piece of silver.'

"The officer assisting the king said to the man of God, 'That couldn't happen even if the Lord opened the windows of heaven!'

"But Elisha replied, 'You will see it happen with your own eyes, but you won't be able to eat any of it!'" (2 Kings 7:1-2 NLT)

My husband and I were going through some difficult financial times with lay-offs and a tough real estate market. Our mortgage (around $2,000) was due on our property, and I needed it within 24 hours or the bank would start foreclosure procedures. I heard a message from my pastor on God, the 24-hour miracle worker. After hearing the message, I went home and fell on my knees that night.

The next day, I read 2 Kings 7:1-2 and prayed to God for a 24-hour miracle. When I read and prayed the next day, I also told God I needed to take the check to the bank in three days. At that moment, I felt the Spirit leading me to go to the mailbox. When I went, nothing was there. So, the second day, I read and prayed the same thing and the Spirit led me to go to the mailbox again and nothing was there. On the third day, I read the scripture, prayed, and declared that He was a 24-hour miracle working God and expressed the need to take the check to my bank tomorrow. Again, the Spirit told me to go to the mailbox.

I said within myself, "This is the third time, but I will obey His leading."

When I went to the mailbox, I saw an envelope from a credit card company. I almost threw it in the trash because I thought they were offering me more credit.

I said, "God, surely you are not going to have me use a new credit card to do this."

But when I looked at the envelope closer, it had the address of the credit card company that I was laid off from three years before. Inside the envelope was a check for $6000! Praise God! They had a letter attached to the check explaining that they audited my layoff package I had accepted and realized that they owed me more money. Oh, my God. How did the company know I would need this money in 24 hours? They didn't, but God knew and He did it in 24 hours. He not only provided for my need, but also blessed me with triple the amount … exceeding my expectations.

"Now to Him who is able to do exceedingly abundantly above all that we ask or think, according to the power that works in us." (Ephesians 3:20 NKJV)

Thank God for His providential and supernatural provision!

My name is Anita,
and I am a JESUS Girl.

At 2 am on January 18, 1994, my life changed forever. My older sister was stabbed to death in the basement of our home while we were sleeping. The killer was a man close to the family. We were shaken to the core. Not just from losing a daughter or sister but also the reality that it could've been us if we hadn't woken up.

At just ten years of age, I faced fear, distrust, self-blame, unforgiveness, and depression, just to name a few. It got to the point where I was having panic attacks. I didn't have anyone I could go to because everyone around me was also grieving. My family believed in God and we knew that He would bring us through. Yet, I was bottling up my emotions and pretending everything was okay since my family was in the public eye, having to deal with the press and media.

While pretending to be okay, I was blaming myself. A couple of months before she was murdered, the man that killed her pulled a knife on me and I didn't tell a soul. As years went on, I battled depression and guilt, and even tried to commit suicide. The enemy got in my mind. I started to believe I was unloved, everything was my fault, and that I was worthless. I had the pills in my hand and as I was about to put them in my mouth, I heard God's voice which stopped me immediately. Even after hearing His voice, I still had trauma from my sister's death to deal with. I refused to get involved in any relationship. I never allowed males to get close to me. I feared the possibility of someone hurting my family or myself.

During my junior year of college, I knew God was healing my heart from the pain, hurt and brokenness. During this time, God gave me the grace to forgive myself and also the man that murdered my sister. With help, I located his address in prison and wrote to him. I certainly did not expect an apology from him, but I needed to say, "I forgive you." He wrote back without an apology and still denied his guilt.

It was only by God's grace that I did not become bitter or angry. I am at peace. God has given me comfort so I can talk about my sister without sorrow. I miss her so much, yet I have joy knowing she is with the Father. I no longer get stuck in that moment when she died. I am thankful for many great memories that I shared with her.

Knowing and feeling God's love, I am no longer afraid to be in a relationship or let people get close to me. I know one day I will be married and have children. I am so thankful God kept me when I didn't want to keep myself. I am grateful, that He saw purpose in me when I thought I was worthless.

I am Anonymous,
and I am a JESUS Girl.

Before God delivered me, my life was filled with so much turmoil. I grew up as a pastor's daughter and was held to an unusually high standard which caused me to be extremely self-critical and self-deprecating. When I could not meet my or other's expectations of perfection, I punished myself. In addition, I was molested at the age of eight. This spun my world into a deep, dark pit of perversion, filled with confusion and addiction for the next nineteen years. I started drinking and smoking weed at twelve to dull the pain. I became addicted to pornography and prescription medications. I also began cutting myself to divert the pain I felt inside. I even started having sexual relationships with both women and men.

I thought that I could fix all of this myself, so I was never transparent with anyone. I self-medicated and self-diagnosed. Eventually, I landed in a psychiatric ward. Some of the people around me thought hospitalization would make me feel better, but it did not help at all. I walked away taking five different medications and numb to the world around me. In order to counteract the numbness, I considered the possibility of a romantic relationship. I thought someone else loving me would fix me. In my attempt to have a relationship, I settled for meeting up with someone I barely knew and got raped. It took a long while for me to process what happened, but when I did, I was shattered.

I knew I needed help but had no clue how to get it. I tried counselors and psychiatrists, but when I left their offices, I felt the same. One day, I was reading a book about trauma and there was a chapter on unforgiveness. As soon as I saw the word, I shut the book. I never wanted to read it again. I felt as if no one deserved my forgiveness. The next Sunday, I went to church and the pastor started talking about how we need to forgive those who hurt us. I just burst into tears and refused to say anything.

A week or so later, someone told me about a healing conference outside of Chicago. I was not working at the time and had no money to go. However, I told God that if He wanted me to go, He would have to make a way. About fifteen minutes later, that person called me back and said they paid for everything so I could go. The conference was not at all what I expected. It was so different from anything I had ever experienced.

On the second day, the speaker said, "Is there anyone here who would feel nauseous at the thought of a certain person walking into the room?" My heart sank and I knew exactly what she meant. She was getting ready to talk about the importance of forgiveness. I started to weep bitterly. I knew the entire church could hear me, but I felt I had no control over my tears. After the end of the session, I went up to receive prayer for trauma and unforgiveness. As a young woman prayed for me, I began weeping again. I wanted to move and run, but I could not. My feet felt as if they were bolted to the floor.

As I began releasing the trauma and the people who hurt me, the Lord opened my eyes. I saw a woman who looked like me rise out of my body and disappear. That was the old me! God delivered me immediately and I never went back to perversion or addiction again. I left with a fire for God and a desire for Him in the most intimate way. God is so amazing and faithful! He has been increasing my desire for Him and intimacy with Him ever since.

My name is Amber,
and I am a JESUS Girl.

Marriage is a blessed thing, but marrying the one God intended is everlasting love. At nineteen years old, I married for the first time without hearing from the Lord. Honestly, I even convinced myself that what I was doing would make God happy. I had sex with my first husband before we were married. He was the one I gave my virginity to. I believed marrying him was the only way to recompense that sexual sin. In reality, Christ desired to give me the husband He created for me from the beginning.

Mistakenly, I thought the fascination we shared was God's invitation for us to marry. It was only a soul tie, created by having sex before marriage. I had an emptiness only Christ could fill. I filled it with a man instead of The Man (Jesus). Looking back, my only job was to plant a seed of the Gospel of Jesus Christ in my ex's life, and move on. Instead, my ex and I formed a relationship that Christ had not intended. Being led by my guilt and lust, I convinced myself that it was Jesus. Sharing the love of Christ with another was all I should've done. Instead I chose to share my bed, my body, and my heart. After dating for three years and married for nine, we divorced.

While going through divorce, I fell head over heels in love with Jesus. Christ began to confront issues in my heart. He pruned, uprooted, and utterly destroyed any sin-nature left in me. It was and still is a beautiful process of transformation.

After my divorce, the Lord revealed my current husband in a vision. He was a friend of mine, someone who I respected like a brother but nothing more. I was satisfied in Christ, content with being single, not even looking for a husband. I was relishing Jesus. However, I surrendered to His will, and my response was, "Not my will be done Lord, but let Your will be done."

I said, "God you are going to have to reveal to him that I am his wife, I am not saying anything!"

I believe a woman should be pursued by her Christ-given husband, not the other way around. Soon after, Christ revealed to my current husband that I was to be his wife.

The love we share is hard to put into words; it's eternal, ecstatic and full of Christ. Our heavenly Father is the ultimate matchmaker. He knows all including who He created to be our mate. While earthly marriage is great, Christ is more concerned with our marriage to Him. He desires a Bride who will love Him more than anyone else. If He happens to give us an earthly mate, well that's nice too. I am extremely thankful for mine! Nevertheless, Jesus will always be my first love.

My name is Brittany,
and I am a JESUS Girl.

———————————

My testimony is not just about the goodness of the Lord but also of His faithful grace upon grace and willingness to give it again and again. In 2003, I discovered a lump in my left breast. Although I didn't want to believe the worst, I went to the doctor and received a diagnosis worse than I imagined. Not only was it cancer, it was a form of cancer the expert surgeon had not seen in thirty years. He wasn't quite sure how he would treat it.

He decided to perform a lumpectomy and was pleased because it appeared he had gotten it all. He said it was contained and the edges around all the tissue he removed were clear of cancer cells. I thanked and praised God for every good report after every mammogram for ten years. Then in 2013, it recurred. It was in the same place at almost the exact same time of the first finding, during the holiday seasons.

I had moved to a new state with new doctors and a surgeon who, just like the first surgeon, was not sure what to do with this reoccurrence. They went ahead and followed the same lumpectomy procedure as the first surgeon. All was well until 2016 when it came back again. Not only was I faced with hearing this diagnosis for the third time, but it came from a new doctor and a new surgeon since my former surgeon had retired.

Though I was weak, He is strong! Because of the multiple occurrences, my doctors and surgeon agreed that a mastectomy was best. The recovery was long and challenging. As soon as I was getting back to some sense of normalcy, my mother passed just two years after the passing of my father.

His grace is sufficient because in 2017, almost one year to the date since the last occurrence, it returned again for a fourth time in the same breast. This meant another surgery and an even longer recovery. God has promised to cure me and I believe I am cured. Throughout this journey I've learned He's a "do it again" God and grants us grace upon grace. There is always new grace to replace the old grace along this journey. I am here by His grace.

My name is Kavetta,
and I am a JESUS Girl.

A few years ago, I was dating this amazing guy. Little did I know he was cheating on me. When I found out, I felt angry and betrayed. I had wasted my time. I was trying to give him a chance and he was playing me. The anger and bitterness didn't go away at all. I was a believer in Christ and attended church. I knew I was supposed to forgive him. I even actively worked on forgiving him, but I couldn't seem to let it go. Sometimes I even said I did, but certain things would happen that let me know I really hadn't forgiven him yet.

If I saw his car, my heart would race and I'd feel angry. If I heard about him or a story about someone else that was similar to what happened to me, I would get angry all over again. The idea of him just agitated me. I knew feeling like that wasn't right, but I didn't know how to make it stop hurting.

A few years later, I began to attend Christ For All Nations Church in Belleville, Illinois and the Lord began a major work in me. The love I experienced there was amazing. Between God's presence in that atmosphere, and the Christ-filled friends He gave me, I was being undone from the inside out. I began to learn more and more about the true love of God. God's love was healing the hurt and anger in me. I began getting into the Word more and surrendering to God in many areas of my life. Through this, my faith started growing stronger.

I knew God was doing a work in me behind the scenes, and one day I was able to see this in action. I was at an event and my ex-boyfriend showed up. When I first saw him, I started laughing, thinking God had a sense of humor. Then I had an epiphany of freedom. Instantly, I realized that where I normally would feel bitter and resentful by seeing him, I sincerely felt God's love for him in my heart. Seeing him didn't bother me anymore. I didn't have images of punching, tripping, or even running him over with my car, so I was like, "Wow, God!"

I felt empowered and even taller in that moment. I knew God had done a work on my heart and was showing me the end result. God's love is so amazing. He forgave me after I hurt Him with my sins, and then He helped me forgive this man for hurting me. God has taught me to not only forgive, but to forgive quickly, and it's all by His grace. If you need help with forgiveness, just surrender and ask God to help you. Learn about His love and let it heal you.

I am Anonymous,
and I am a JESUS Girl.

As a young girl, I learned about the Lord and was saved. As I grew older, I realized that I didn't have a true relationship with God. My life centered around me and not Him. Though I was going to church regularly and presented Him as "head" of my life, something was missing. I continued my façade of religion until I was faced with the worst of nightmares.

I lost it all. My career, my apartment, my husband, my life, my future, and a big part of my faith were gone. After turning to family and friends to help me, I realized I stopped believing and trusting the One who had never forsaken me and never let me down.

I needed to do something different and fast. I prayed. Not just regular prayer, but a meaningful, specific, continuous prayer. I had to be specific with God. General prayer yields general results. Intentional prayer yields intentional results. I realized the first thing I needed to pray about was trust. Can you believe such a small word has so much strength and power in our lives? If you don't trust something or someone, your approach is different, your thoughts are different, and your actions are different.

I didn't trust God the way I should and needed to trust Him. Looking at my life, knowing He would never forsake me or any of us, how is that even possible? Easy, we are human. Years of disappointment, sadness, abuse (verbal and physical), and trauma clouded my understanding and most importantly, my faith. So I prayed an intentional, specific prayer to God seeking trust and He delivered.

However, His delivery came with some hard lessons, hard times, and difficult seasons. I needed all of it. Every lesson, circumstance, trial and tribulation taught me that if and when I feel I have nothing else, I have a faithful God. It's hard trusting when you are having a hard time but what I've learned is sometimes God has to take you *through* some things to get you to where He wants you to be.

After that prayer, God took me through a season of learning to trust Him. He showed up in every situation. Not only did He teach me how to trust Him, He also taught me that He literally holds everything and everybody in His hands.

This one particular event really blew me away. God called me to put together a prayer breakfast for little girls, called "God's Precious Jewels". I was amazed He would even ask me. In the past, I would stress and try to figure it all out but God showed up and provided everything, and I mean everything! From the food to the decor, the gifts, the volunteers, and even the venue!

Without telling anyone, I envisioned this particular location in my mind. All of a sudden, the person over that building reached out to me about the event and inquired if I had a place yet. I told her I didn't and she offered their facility! I was shocked. Even when I set my expectations low, thinking just a few girls would attend, God exceeded my own thoughts and more than tripled the attendance. God provided everything and everyone and blew my mind. This was my first time really experiencing God on a new level. The event reminded me that He is a trustworthy provider. So keep your purpose, keep your hope, keep your faith, and keep trust in the Lord our God for He is worthy!

I am Anonymous,
and I am a JESUS Girl.

Growing up, there was always a wedge between my mother and I. It became such an issue that I left home and joined the army in search of love and freedom. I always dreamed of being a wife and mother of six driving the minivan to my job, church and home that we would own. Reality was very different. For many years, I lived a very promiscuous life not thinking of anyone but myself.

I married my first husband while with child from another man. While married, I had two more children but then the relationship ended in divorce. I married my second husband still looking for acceptance and love but instead it was filled with both physical and mental abuse. I entered this marriage with child, lost another child and bore my last baby.

As the years went on, the physical abuse became worse. Once he pushed me into our deadlocked back door. The key went through the bridge of my nose. My husband dropped me off at the emergency room and left me there alone. I ended up with six stitches and two black eyes.

During this difficult marriage, I began reading the Bible. I knew that what my husband told me about the Lord, church, and myself could not be right. I grew up in the church but never took God seriously. I knew God would not have created me for nothing.

I ended up staying with this husband for fourteen years. I was afraid to leave because I wouldn't have any help raising my five children. I also was embarrassed because this was my second marriage. I knew it looked bad for me and the family name. So I read my Bible, went back to school and got a good paying job. This too came at a price. I had to deal with him each night when I got home.

I started saving and preparing for my get away. I would sneak clothes and money out of the house and store them in my cabinet at work. Sadly, I never made that getaway. Instead, he sensed me pulling away and things just got worse. My daughter called the police after his last attack on both me and my oldest daughter.

My third husband was a charm. It lasted a total of nine months from the time we dated until his death. He died of a massive aneurysm which surprised everyone including me.

Through multiple divorces, raising children, and even sometimes unemployment, God has kept me. There was a time when we had no food and my neighbors came over and fed the dogs who lived outside. They never did knock on the door to see if the family needed anything. But, God provided. Once my dad happened to stop by on his way home. Someone had given him some deer meat. He said he had more than enough already in his freezer at home and left it with me. That night I made "macadeer", at least that's what the kids and I called it.

Finally, at a time when I least expected it, I met my current husband. I was happy for the most part but felt unworthy of God's love and didn't accept the blessing He had given me. I felt as though my past determined my worth. I had just started selling Avon and was a vendor at a Jesus Girl conference. I expected to make money but never expected to find God or to learn He had already forgiven me for my transgressions.

I now seek God first in everything I do. I can now receive the love my husband has for me, more than I could ever imagine. We are now part of Christ's body and walk in faith together. I am at peace.

I am Kim,
and I am a JESUS Girl.

God is so good to me. Recently I celebrated my 66th birthday and realized I have been saved for fifty years. That's half a century. Oh, my goodness. If I tell you that I'm the only person left in my immediate family, you might think I'm lonely. Not so. My only child died at the age of 24 in December 1998 after being in a head-on collision. He left behind his wife and two young daughters. Then, my mother went on to glory on Valentine's Day 2016. In His love and grace, my loving God has surrounded me with lots of very loving godchildren (I have seven plus their families).

My God-given family consists of my special niece and her family who insist I eat dinner with them every Sunday, my church family, my hairdresser and her family, my godmother and her son, and the "Fabulous Five" ladies whose husbands also lived in Japan and Hawaii while we were there. I am never, ever lonely! I see God's hand in everything that happens to and for me the more I put my trust in Jesus. My favorite slogan is "Look at God" as He is consistently handling things for me. I love it so much that it's become my vanity license plate: LKAT GOD. I love Jesus so much and am grateful for the Holy Spirit residing in, leading and guiding me daily.

I am Sandy,
and I am a JESUS Girl.

I used to believe I was born for pain because all of my memories were about me being mistreated and given no love. I grew up in a dope house and was then placed with so many different people who did not want me. At fifteen years old, at 3 pm on a Saturday, I was kidnapped and raped by total strangers. Once I was released, I went back to a house where just hearing laughter from other children made me feel more broken. I never felt any value. I believed I would never receive joy so why live through all this pain.

One night, I was awakened to the sound of my name being called. It surprised me because I had never heard it called correctly before. I believe it was God calling me. It sounded so perfect that the darkness disappeared and my eyes opened. God started my deliverance, healing, and salvation. Before this, I never really gave God a thought but I knew who it was when the almighty God called my name.

I am learning through His sovereignty that God loves me. There is evil in the land but God has created us and John says, "*I am come that they might have life, and that they might have it more abundantly.*" (John 10:10 KJV) I have seen and experienced a lot of devastation but through it all, Jesus has kept my mind and that's my biggest testimony. I lost my mind trying take my life but God has given me a strong mind of love and grace and compassion for all people. I won't let the devil win.

So, hold on and you will see the grace of God.

I am Lane,
and I am a JESUS Girl.

In the early 90s, I relocated from San Diego to Hollywood in pursuit of my dream to become a famous dancer and choreographer. During that time, I landed work as a backup dancer for Kurtis Blow for an event called Rapmania, his live concert celebrating the 15th anniversary of hip hop. The event brought together some of the most influential rap artists.

During this event, I began living the Hollywood hip hop music industry lifestyle. I met and hooked up with one of the artists in the show. Things moved quickly. Not long into the relationship, I found out I was pregnant. Shortly after, being young, naïve and clueless, I moved in with him. I had no idea what I got myself into but I knew for sure I was lost.

Years later, I survived what is now known as the Northridge Earthquake of 1994 with a magnitude of 6.6- 6.7 on the Richter scale. It violently shook the city of Los Angeles and left much of it in ruins with buildings and freeways collapsed. During the quake, we lived in a high-rise apartment building. I could literally hear the nails in the wood popping and cracking as the building shook violently.

Overwhelmed with fear, a revelation suddenly came to me, "If I die, I'll be separated from God and spend eternity in hell." I was not a religious person, however, instinctively in that moment- I cried out "LORD, SAVE ME. I don't want to die." Days following the quake, I had a supernatural encounter with God that changed the course of my life.

I heard a voice say, "Kenyetta, go get your Bible."

Although I was reluctant at first, I felt prompted to find it. Much to my amazement, the book opened right to, *"And the Lord said, 'If ye had faith as a grain of mustard seed'"* (Luke 17:6a KJV). That caught my attention. I recalled my grandma saying that but I had no idea she was quoting scripture. I just assumed she made it up. Before I knew it, I felt a presence enter the room. I immediately recognized it was the Lord and it frightened me.

He said, "Be not afraid. It is I, and I am with you."

The fear left. I asked Him the purpose of this visit. He said, "It's time you got your life right with Me and your kids need to know Me."

As we talked, I noticed when I would ask a question, He would always answer. When I would look down at the Bible, it would be turned to a specific page and the verse would stand out like 3D coming off the pages.

I asked one last question, "How do I know You're the way?"

His response was *"I am the way, the truth, and the life: no man cometh unto the Father, but by me."* (John 14:6b KJV)

I shared this experience with a family member who invited me to church to meet with her pastor.

I will never forget what he said to me, "Young lady, God has a plan for your life."

He prayed with me and I gave my life to the Lord vowing to serve Him all the days of my life.

My name is Kenyetta,
and I am a JESUS Girl.

After living in Georgia for about eight years, I came home to St. Louis. I was alone with no family members in Georgia, yet, I loved it there and really didn't think I would move back to St. Louis. I thought I was just coming home for the birth of my great grandchild. Little did I know God was setting me up to be blessed.

My job transferred me with a better position. I was told I could live in a close friend's home who passed away. She had been like a sister to me. Her daughter (my niece) said it was occupied at the time so I lived with both my daughters until I found my own place. I was very happy to be on my own again. Meanwhile, I was losing weight and getting tired much more than normal.

About one month into living in my beautiful condo, my niece called to tell me the house was empty and if I still wanted to move in, I could. I struggled with the decision so I called prayer partners because I didn't understand why this would open up after I had just moved. I decided to move into the house and as soon as I did, I found myself under a financial attack. Thankfully, I was in a home that was paid for. Shortly after that, my health was attacked.

I didn't know what was going on with me so I told my girls, "If this doesn't get better, I will go get a checkup."

It didn't get better so I kept my word. I went to the emergency room for a checkup. After being examined, the doctor and three nurses came into the room.

The doctor asked, "How did you get here?"

I told him, "I drove."

He asked, "Are you dizzy?" and about other symptoms.

I said, "No."

He said, "I don't know how you're standing there with no symptoms. You are severely anemic, you have no blood, and you need a transfusion ASAP."

He started showing me the outward signs to look for. I had them, but I was not affected by them. He admitted me with orders for a blood transfusion starting with three pints. I ended up with four. The doctor said I had to have more tests so they could find out why I was losing so much blood. I made an appointment for an upper and lower GI which brought more bad news. They found cancer (God had me call it a situation, so I did) in my colon.

I had to take time off work to have surgery, but because I lived in a paid-for home, I could not get unemployment. My paperwork was not in for worker's comp so I had no income. But God! Not only did He deliver me from that situation, every bill was paid while I was off work for five months.

God put people in my life that blessed me. I was sitting in my bedroom talking to my oldest sister who came to check on me. After she left, I got a phone call from a friend who said, "I'm just checking on you and by the way, give me your landlord's address. I want to pay your rent." As

I was crying and thanking God for the blessing, I called my sister and told her how God had just blessed me.

She said, "That's so good, sis. Now look under your pillow."

All I saw were hundred-dollar bills. I must have cried that whole day thanking God because I know where my help comes from. Needless to say, He met every need and some wants. I thank God. I love God. I loved Him before the situation and more after the situation. Thank you, Father, for being so good to me. God brought me home to be a blessing and also to be blessed.

My name is Annette,
and I am a JESUS Girl.

At a tender age, all I wanted was someone to love me and encourage me to love myself. I really did not know what love entailed, but I was searching for it. I was born out of wedlock to teenage parents and I was raised by my hardworking grandmother. My dad had another child three months after my birth and he decided to stay with that mother instead. They had nine other children together. This left me with real daddy issues. I felt abandoned, unloved, and rejected. It was like I was standing outside looking through the window at their family and not being asked to come in. I did not spend much time with my siblings until I was old enough to pursue them on my own, and even then, it was awkward. So I began searching to find my own family to love.

At seven years of age, I started going to church with my neighbors. They had a daughter about twelve years old. I was very excited to be learning about this man named Jesus. I loved it! By the time I was eleven, I was helping teach preschoolers on Sunday, read church announcements, do some work in the office, and sing in the choir. We even made an album. I was so grateful to be part of something. I had a sense of belonging there. Even though I was going to church, my foundation was not really rooted and grounded in the Lord yet. I was barely a teen when the enemy came in the form of perversion, lust, manipulation, and deception, right there in the church. I spiraled out of control quickly, leaving the church, and going into the wilderness to be sifted.

I started drinking, experimenting with drugs, and hanging out with the wrong people. Before I turned thirty, I had two sons and three DUI's. Alcohol became my new family. I had numerous car accidents. One accident landed me at the bottom of an overpass, leaving me in a coma for a week. When I woke up, I asked for a doctor. I had to tell him that my finger was broken.

Despite all this, the Lord was on my side and He put Psalm 51 on my heart. God showed me that I may have left the church, but He never left me. Little did I know before I was born, I was set apart and God had a plan for me. Because of Christ, today, I am ten years clean and sober.

In my fifth year of sobriety, I lost my youngest son to a car accident due to bad weather conditions. He was twenty-one. Glory to God the Father, He kept me clean and sober, and gave me peace during my loss. Six weeks later, a spirit of cancer hit my family and took my aunt. She was diagnosed on the same day that my son died. Within the next year, I lost three more family members to cancer, only six months after the last death. Still, God kept me sober. Then, only three years ago, I was diagnosed with stage four, small cell cancer.

The doctor said, "I can make you comfortable".

This was only my first appointment, and I told him "But God!"

The doctor was trying to deliver a death sentence, but God has given me life, and I'm still here! It was during this time, I realized how much the Lord truly loves me. I had finally found what I was looking for – love, His love. *"The Lord is my light and my salvation; whom shall I fear?"* (Psalm 27:1a KJV). I thank the Lord, for teaching me His ways and precepts and I thank Him for His Word that fills my heart.

My name is Betrina,
and I am a JESUS Girl.

My name is Maria, my friends and family call me Mita, and God calls me His daughter. I am a grieving mother that got up! I lost my son, (Devon Marquis Graham, 20 years old) on June 30, 2019 to suicide. I will never forget that day when my life changed forever. The grief, desperation, and sadness overtook me. My days were full of tears, confusion, blame, anxiety, and darkness. I didn't want to get up, I didn't want to go out, and I didn't want to continue...but God.

On September 19, 2019, I decided to listen to that voice within me telling me to get up. Get up! Get out of bed! Open the curtains! Through this profound pain, God used me to be His voice. He gave me the strength to share my story and used me to encourage others because He knew if I could just get up, He would use my pain to bring forth deliverance. Deliverance from depression, deliverance from despair.

Today, I choose to get up!

My name is Maria,
and I am a JESUS Girl.

ENDNOTES

CHAPTER ONE

1. Genesis 29:15 NLT
2. Genesis 29:16
3. Genesis 29:17
4. Genesis 29:18-19
5. Genesis 29:20
6. Genesis 29:21
7. Genesis 29:25
8. Genesis 29:26-28
9. Genesis 29:31 KJV
10. Genesis 29:32 ESV
11. Genesis 29:34 NKJV
12. Genesis 29:35 CEB

CHAPTER TWO

1. 1 Samuel 1:10a
2. 1 Samuel 1:7
3. 1 Samuel 1:8b KJV
4. 1 Samuel 1:6

5. Psalm 47:7
6. 1 Samuel 1:5b
7. 1 Samuel 1:19b
8. Galatian 6:9
9. 1 Samuel 2:21a
10. Proverbs 17:22a

CHAPTER THREE

1. https://www.lexico.com/en/definition/loyal
2. https://www.lexico.com/en/definition/wisdom
3. https://www.lexico.com/en/definition/peacemaker
4. Forrest Gump. Hollywood, CA: Paramount Pictures, 2001.

CHAPTER FOUR

1. https://www.google.com/search?ei=rXuGXu-ABO-wtgW2zK-PICw&q=prepared+definition&oq=prepared+de&gs_lcp=Cg-Zwc3ktYWIQAxgAMgIIADICCAAyAggAMgIIADICCAAy-AggAMgIIADICCAAyAggAMgIIADoECAAQR1DNWl-jeW2DnZmgAcAN4AIABTogBgQGSAQEymAEAoAEBqgE-HZ3dzLXdpeg&sclient=psy-ab
2. https://www.merriam-webster.com/dictionary/prepared

CHAPTER FIVE

1. Kadari, Tamar. "Gomer, daughter of Diblaim: Midrash and Aggadah." *Jewish Women: A Comprehensive Historical Encyclopedia*. 27 February 2009. Jewish Women's Archive. (Viewed on March 26, 2020) <https://jwa.org/encyclopedia/article/gomer-daughter-of-diblaim-midrash-and-aggadah>.
2. Ibid

3. https://www.biblegateway.com/resources/
   all-women-bible/Gomer
4. John 3:16b NIV
5. "Prostitution." *Merriam-Webster*, Merriam-Webster, Oct.
   17, 2019. https://www.merriam-webster.com/dictionary/
   prostitution.

CHAPTER SIX

1. Luke 1:28b NIV
2. Luke 1:34 NIV
3. Luke 1:38 NIV
4. https://www.gotquestions.org/count-the-cost.html?fbclid=I-
   wAR1Aa_u6V48uHr6NrrX52I3mfxSbDgnV2jl2PFhGbog7G-
   jsxFD_iIJ-xEC4

CHAPTER SEVEN

1. Joanna "The Woman Who, Healed by Christ,
   Honored Him."
2. (2019, August 29). Retrieved from Bible Gateway:
3. www.biblegateway.com/resources/all-women-bible/Joanna

CHAPTER EIGHT

1. Luke 8:43-48 TPT
2. Leviticus 15:25-27 NLT
3. Lexico Online Dictionary
4. Psalm 63:1-8 TPT
5. Acts 17:28 NIV
6. Luke 8:47 TPT
7. Psalm 40:8 NKJV

JESUS GIRL TESTIMONIES

1. *"Through It All Lyrics." Lyrics.com.* STANDS4 LLC, 2019. Web. 17 Oct. 2019. https://www.lyrics.com/lyric/847594/ Andra%C3%A9+Crouch.

2. 1 Corinthians 15:31b (KJV) *paraphrased*

3. Galatians 2:20 *paraphrased*

4. *"My Testimony Lyrics." Lyrics.co* STANDS4 LLC, 2019. Web. 17 Oct. 2019. <https://www.lyrics.com/lyric/28767016/ Marvin+Sapp>.

WORKS CITED

Bloom, J. (2011, August 19). *Desiring God.* Retrieved from Judas Was The Treasurer?: www.desiringgod.org/articles/judas-was-the-treasurer

https://www.biblegateway.com/ passage/?search=genesis+29&version=CEB

"Desperate, Adj. 2." Lexico Online Dictionary, Lexico, 2019,

Easton, Matthew. "Joanna - Easton's Bible Dictionary." Blue Letter Bible. 24 Jun, 1996. Web. 26 Mar, 2020. <https://www.blueletter-bible.org/search/Dictionary/viewTopic.cfm>.

https://www.lexico.com/en/definition/desperate

Fletcher, E. (2006). *Women in the Bible.* Retrieved from Joanna, Jesus' disciple, gospel woman: www.womeninthebible.net/ women-bible-old-new-testaments/joanna/

Forrest Gump. Hollywood, CA: Paramount Pictures, 2001.

"Gomer – All the Women of the Bible". Bible Gateway. Zondervan. 1988. Oct. 17, 2019. Biblegateway.com/resources/all-women-bible/Gomer

Hitchcock, Roswell. "Gomer - Hitchcock's Bible Names Dictionary." Blue Letter Bible. 24 Jun, 1996. Web. 26 Mar, 2020. <https://www.blueletterbible.org/search/Dictionary/viewTopic.cfm>.

Hitchcock, Roswell. "Joanna - Hitchcock's Bible Names Dictionary." Blue Letter Bible. 24 Jun, 1996. Web. 26 Mar, 2020. <https://www.blueletterbible.org/search/Dictionary/viewTopic.cfm>.

https://www.biblegateway.com/passage/?search=leviticus+15&version=NLT

Joanna "The Woman Who, Healed by Christ, Honored Him. (2019, August 29). Retrieved from Bible Gateway: www.biblegateway.com/resources/all-women-bible/Joanna

Kadari, Tamar. "Gomer, daughter of Diblaim: Midrash and Aggadah." *Jewish Women: A Comprehensive Historical Encyclopedia.* 27 February 2009. Jewish Women's Archive. (Viewed on March 26, 2020) <https://jwa.org/encyclopedia/article/gomer-daughter-of-diblaim-midrash-and-aggadah>.

King, K. L. (1998, April). *Frontline.* Retrieved from Women In Ancient Christianity: The New Discoveries: www.pbs.org/wgbh/pages/frontline/shows/religion/first/women

"Like Mother, Like Daughter." Farlex Dictionary of Idioms. 2015. Farlex, Inc. Oct. 17, 2019. https://idioms.thefreedictionary.com/like+mother%2c+like+daughter

"Loyal." Lexico.com, Oxford University Press (OUP), 2019, https://www.lexico.com/definition/loyal

"My Testimony Lyrics." *Lyrics.com.* STANDS4 LLC, 2019. Web. 17 Oct. 2019. https://www.lyrics.com/lyric/28767016/Marvin+Sapp.

https://www.biblegateway.com/passage/?search=psalm+40&version=NKJV

"Peacemaker." Lexico.com, Oxford University Press (OUP), 2019, https://www.lexico.com/definition/peacemaker

"Prostitution." *Merriam-Webster*, Merriam-Webster, Oct. 17, 2019. https://www.merriam-webster.com/dictionary/prostitution.

"Prostrate." *Merriam-Webster*, Merriam-Webster, Oct. 17, 2019. https://www.merriam-webster.com/dictionary/prostrate

https://www.biblegateway.com/passage/?search=luke+8&version=TPT

"What does it mean to "count the cost" (Luke 14:28)?" *Got Questions*, Got Questions Ministries, Sept.10, 2019. https://www.gotquestions.org/count-the-cost.html.

https://www.biblegateway.com/passage/?search=genesis+29&version=ESV

"Through It All Lyrics." *Lyrics.com.* STANDS4 LLC, 2019. Web. 17 Oct. 2019. https://www.lyrics.com/lyric/847594/Andra%C3%A9+Crouch.

"What does it mean to "count the cost" (Luke 14:28)?.GotQuestions.org. https://www.gotquestions.org/count-the-cost.html.

"Wisdom." Lexico.com, Oxford University Press (OUP), 2019, https://www.lexico.com/definition/wisdom

McCrave, Jerry. 2020. JESUS Girl. Jerry McCrave Photography, Jerry.McCrave@gmail.com

Made in the USA
Monee, IL
03 September 2020